The Hunter-Gatherer Way

THE HUNTER-GATHERER WAY

Putting back the apple

Ffyona Campbell

Wild Publishing

In loving memory of my mother
Angela Rosemary Campbell

and

For my beautiful daughter
Elsa
my sunshine song

About the Author

Ffyona Campbell was born in Totnes, Devon, in 1967. She spent many years exploring the world from on foot and, as she went, learning from Australian Aborigines, African Bushmen, Pygmies, and North American Indians. In 1997 she returned home to learn the wild food of her native land and to find out what had happened to us, 4,000 years ago, to turn us away from the hunter-gatherer life we loved. Since then she has taught over 1,000 people how to be hunter-gatherers here in Britain.

By the same author

Feet of Clay, a walk across Australia (Orion)
On Foot Through Africa, a walk the length of Africa (Orion)
The Whole Story, a walk around the world (Orion)

Acknowledgements

Thank you to all my family for your encouragement; to my wonderful friends for our nourishing conversations through thick and thin; to the many hundreds of people who have come on my wild food walks - when all of you were amazed too, I knew I was on the right track; and to the members of the Ffyona Campbell Appreciation Society whose determination to bring me back overcame those who had made me never want to connect with the world again.

But most of all, thank you to my daughter Elsa, for all the times you've had to wait "til I've finished writing something down", ever since you were two years old. Thank you for reminding me what it's all about; without you, life would have been a very empty page.

Praise for The Hunter-Gatherer Way

"I loved every single page of this book. It was an enriching experience and felt like a privilege to read it. A pure glow is present in the writing." *Tom Jones, London*

"The best piece of female intuitive writing I have ever read. Nobody has written a book like this. The thinking is as clear as a mountain stream." *Phil Sheardown, Canoe Adventures, Totnes*

"I am simply nourished to read this book. It feeds my soul." *Laura Newman, Infinity Parenting, Totnes*

"An extraordinarily perceptive, intelligent and intuitive book." *Miranda Day, MA (hons) Oxford*

"This book is a little treasure, a refreshing gem of intuitive insight and reflection, a pleasure to read and a wonderful contribution as we all tread our own individual and collective wild journeys." Fergus Drennan, *Wild Man, Wild Food*

"Quite simply it is an authentic voice of a deeply intuitive, thoughtful individual who has carried her share of burden the better to attach herself to mother earth with a straight back and a clear gaze into the future. It is also – importantly – a book for men, written by a woman. There are some uncomfortable ideas that need to be accommodated in man-dom." Rory MacPhee, Falassa, Cornwall

"Part 4: The Ring of the Wild Food Year has just blown me away. So beautifully written, it speaks to my heart and stirs my wildest (lifestyle) fantasies! I long to have your knowledge and skills." *Jax Higginson*

"A *fantastic* read! The writing is as fresh as a shower of rain. Ffyona has a unique way of facilitating and empowering people to think in a different way." *Simone Wilkie, artist, Shatkiart, Totnes*

"This book is an absolute triumph because it moves our understanding of history away from the world of speculative academic theory into a new paradigm of intuitive and rational understanding. All those history professors around the world must be quaking in their ivory towers to see how you have cleared the fog with your bright rays of common sense!!" *Greg Meanwell, Homeopath, Totnes*

"The images in The Ring of the Wild Food Year, are so beautiful." *Francis Deutsch, small-holder, Totnes*

"It's so full of original thought. Most books you read will have some new ideas but mostly you'll have heard a lot of it before. But this book is original thought from beginning to end." *Caroline Snow, Stoke Gabriel*

"After reading this book I can feel my hormones coursing through my blood, I feel very juicy with the wisdom I can feel emanating from the words, from the experiences. I need to talk about this and I want to share this with other women. It makes me feel connected. It's a missing link. It makes so much sense.

This book is going to be very, very popular. People will read it and share it and it will become a household name like the Continuum Concept." *Laura Newman, Infinity Parenting, Totnes*

"The Hunter-Gatherer Way, is a rich clear look at our essential nature and the ever nourishing interconnected web of life. A very inspiring and deeply beautiful book, so needed." *Hannah Pearson*

"I read this beautiful work immediately after reading an outback survival guide and found many tangents around respect and living in sync. The Hunter-Gatherer Way is a gentle and down to Earth synergy of keen observations, tested theories and the lost art of commonsense. Thank you for your patience, love and curiosity for all that our Earth offers and willingness to share your valuable wisdom and insight." *Terra'Mer Lalirra*

Contents

Introduction

I've been very fortunate to have found some truly amazing things on my journeys and having shared them with people on my wild food walks, I have been asked so many times to write a book, that I thought I would.

But, I didn't just want to share only the answers, I wanted to explain how I worked them out because it's in the *thinking* and in the kinds of questions you ask yourself, that will enable you too to see through the 4,000 years of progress and development that obscures the way.

It's not hard, we were meant to think like this and once you see how it's done, it all becomes very obvious. No matter where you are in Britain, you can work out how we lived as hunter-gatherers in your area too and so you can apply it to your daily life. Without this knowledge you can't live from wild food all year round because there just isn't enough.

I think of this knowledge as our birthright and hopefully our future and so, in the words of the Cherokee grandmother in Forrest Carter's wonderful book The Education of Little Tree:

"When you come on something good, first thing to do is to share it with whosoever you can find, that way the good spreads out where there's no telling how far it will go."

PART 1

Learning to Think Like a Hunter-Gatherer

1

This journey really began when I first realised there was something to learn. I was sitting by a river in Mali, west Africa, as dusk was falling, several hundred miles from any village and so the animals were not afraid.

A family of baboons came to down to drink on the opposite side of the river and when they had finished, they disappeared into the bush and a family of smaller animals appeared and they drank and disappeared too, and then a family of even smaller ones came, and so on. They came in their kind, bowed their heads and drank, then retreated silently into the bush.

In the middle of the river, large birds swooped down and skimmed the surface of the water with their beaks, then smaller birds flew down, then in the very last of the light, the tiniest birds flew down to drink and then they too flew away into the deepening darkness.

Witnessing this reverent procession, this holy communion, I realised that it had happened every evening and before every dawn since the beginning and that not so long ago, there had been a place for people in it, too. We had once known what it felt like to be no greater and no lesser than anyone else. It gave me such a huge sense of relief when I realised that we don't have to rule the world at all, it works very well, all by itself.

*

When I was walking around the world, through the whole spectrum of human development, I noticed that the happiest, healthiest people I met were the hunter-gatherers: Bushmen and Pygmies, Aborigines and North American Indians. They seemed to have such a lightness of being and such a depth of understanding that I could never see them asking questions like "Why are we here?" or "Who made us?"or "What is the meaning of life?" because they already seemed to know the answers.

So, when the walk was finished, and I was wondering what to do next, I decided to take what I'd earned and go and find out whether they really do have the answers and whether their way of life really is any better than the western way.

But, where to go? I don't really like rainforests having nearly been eaten by one, but I do like deserts. I like the open space, the dry air and the suntan. I find that people who live in deserts are much calmer than those who live in rainforests and so, I decided to go and live with the Aborigines.

I'd had a very special encounter with an Aborigine when I was walking. I'd reached a truck stop on a reserve and I was getting some much needed relief from the heat with a cold coke in the café when some Aborigines had come in. The cashier had stiffened, the little children went straight for the sweets and the adults didn't pay any attention at all to the havoc they were causing.

I finished my coke and went outside to carry on when a young Aborigine man came over to me and asked me if I was the one walking. I said I was. And then he asked me:

"How good is it?" It was the only time anyone ever asked me a question like that and I really liked it. Everyone else seemed to think me very strange. But in that question I felt I was understood.

I explained that it was awful, in fact, because my feet were infected with blisters. He said he'd like to walk to Perth with me and I'd said I wished he would.

I'd said goodbye and thought no more about it. But later, walking through the night to avoid the searing heat, I was hunched over in a painful shuffle trying not to dislodge the blisters and singing to try and cheer myself up when I suddenly realised that I wasn't alone. There were footsteps coming up behind me - in the middle of the desert, in the middle of the night, in the middle of an Aboriginal reserve!

I was so frightened that I just couldn't look round. The person making those footsteps must have sensed my fear because he, or she, stayed just out of my peripheral vision, behind my right shoulder. The footsteps were very rhythmical and relaxed and as I got used to them being there without anything else happening, I realised my own awkward gait had fallen in time with them. The gentle thrumming of those feet allowed me to relax and I felt myself walking upright for the first time in many days.

Over the hours that followed in perfect rhythm, the sun finally came up and I plucked up the courage to look round, but there was nobody there.

Six years and twelve thousand miles later, I returned to Australia. With a friend, Tony Mitchetschlager, who had cycled around the world, I flew to Perth, bought an old Toyota land-cruiser and headed north towards Arnhemland which belongs to the Aborigines.

After a couple of days driving up the desolate highway, we noticed a tiny rusty sign which said "Aboriginal Rock Art 15km" and it pointed down a dirt track. I decided to go and explore this because it would give me a good introduction to their way of life before I met them.

If this was the UK and there were some 40,000 year old rock paintings, there'd have been a car park with an information board, a kiosk taking money and quite possibly an ice-cream van but here, there was nothing. A woman in a truck stop said she'd never seen the rock art herself, didn't know what it looked like either but if we pulled in further down the road it should be around somewhere.

We did pull in down the road and I wracked my brains for any ideas about where the Aborigines might have put some rock art and thought it would be a good idea to start looking up on the highest peaks, nearest the sun because this was supposed to represent the spirits of the animals wasn't it? And that's the sort of thing that people did to honour their spirits, wasn't it?

So we climbed the highest stack of rocks we could find, about an hour's walk from the land-cruiser. The sun bounced incessantly off the bright sandstone surfaces, there was no shade and I felt my chest begin to heave and my breathing get shallower. I'd tried to cool myself down by wetting my skin and turning into the breeze, but there was no wind at all. A deafening thump pounded in my ears. I didn't want to admit it but I knew I was getting heat stroke. Finally, nauseous and unstable, I said I was going back down the rocks to find some shade. Tony said he would continue looking around up there, completely unfazed by the heat.

I reached a dried up river bed and thought that if I followed it 'up stream' I'd find a tree. After a few minutes, I turned a corner and there *was* a tree, far in the distance. I thanked Heaven. Then I noticed that right beside the tree was a patch of shade cast by an overhang of rock.

Heavenly *bliss*!

I managed to get into that shade before I ran out of puff but once I had sat down it took me quite a while to get my breathing under control. I was feeling a bit annoyed with myself that I'd had to bow out and sit in the shade while Tony continued with the hunt. But as my eyes adjusted to the low level of light in there, I realised that I was completely surrounded by Aboriginal rock art.

As I sat there looking at all the drawings of mostly turtles etched into the rock surface, I had to laugh. I'd been operating under the belief that there is a difference between us and the people who made this art because 40,000 years separates us. But this experience was telling me that we are exactly the same now as we were then because our needs haven't changed. We get heat stroke if we stand in the sun. So did they. We feel comfortable on a hot day if we sit in the shade. So did they. And as I stood at the rock-face in the same position as the artist and realised I needed an elbow rest, so had they – there was one right in the most perfect place.

I realised that this discovery was the key to understanding everything. No matter what I was looking for I would find the answers if I just put myself in their shoes and asked myself what *I* would do in this situation? And what *I* would need?

And from then on, I made sure that this line of thinking: that *we have not changed*, was my filter, my guide, my separator of wheat from chaff. My common sense.

Continuing our drive north, we heard about another kind of rock art from a man who taken some photographs. He showed us what he had. They depicted tall, elegant people who appeared to be flying. The man explained they were made by a people who *pre-dated* the Aborigines. Nobody knows anything about them and the Aborigines say it's rubbish art and before their time. They are only found in the Kimberly area of north west Australia.

These rock paintings have been called "The Bradshaws" after the pastoralist Joseph Bradshaw who discovered them in the late 1800's whilst looking for grazing for his cattle. The latest idea, explained the photographer, was that they were made by West Africans because they depict people who are tall and elegant and highly decorated with bangles and necklaces. The theory is that these people had found their way from the east coast of Africa to the west coast of Australia 70,000 years ago.

Hmm. After looking at them, I wasn't so sure. The legs on these people were very short for West Africans.

We asked the photographer where they were but the closest he could get to showing us was on a map. We would have to find them ourselves.

We spent several days in Broome getting the land-cruiser stocked up then headed inland on the unpaved Gibb River road. It crosses the vast dry desert devoid of much greenery or water but every now and again it runs near a deep ravine which, when you look down into it, shows a valley full of tropical plants, splashing waterfalls and butterflies.

After many adventures, we found one of the Bradshaw paintings. It was on a rock, about an hour's drive off the road through the bush. The owner of the cattle station had been kind enough to point us in the general direction and the closer we got to it, the more we scouted around on foot until we found it.

The painting was about a foot high of a young woman, very tall and elegant, bedecked with bangles and little bags. She looked very stylish and quite magical and by the position of her feet off the ground, she appeared to be flying.

We gathered wood and made camp. I wanted to stay for as long as it took to figure out who had made this painting. I realised that to cross the divide of time and culture, I had to be aware of what I was *actually* experiencing because that would be similar to what *she* had experienced. This was the thing we had in common and in there would be the clue.

So, I concentrated acutely on how hot or cold I felt, noticing that I felt hot beside some rocks and cold beside others. I noticed how interesting it is to stand in the shadow of a rock and watch the insects in the sunlight before the sun comes round the corner and blinds you; how the sunlight caught my eyes and made me squint which made me see my eyelashes as rainbow coloured fans; how the smell of plants changed as evening came on and how they smelt differently at night and then how the perfume of dawn was different again as the plants changed their breathing from day to night and back again.

The Bradshaw girl would have experienced all of these things, but none of them was giving me a clue as to who she was or who had painted her portrait, 70,000 years ago.

And then, on the afternoon of the third day, I saw it. I suddenly noticed that my shadow was stretching out long and elegant in front of me. And it had very short legs.

I looked closely at the proportions on the rest of my shadow and realised they aren't the same as those of a person: on a shadow at this time of day, the head is very small and the shoulders are narrow, the arms are super long and if they hang down by your side the hands are very large, the torso is very long but the legs are very short. I went back to the Bradshaw and, sure enough, these were the proportions of the girl in the painting. So, I realised that these aren't paintings of people at all but paintings of people's *shadows*.

And who would be interested in their shadows stretching tall and elegant in front of them? Tall, elegant people like West Africans? No, I didn't think so. How about very short people? Yes, much more likely. I later found out there are a group of Pygmies living not far away on the island of Papua New Guinea who have a highly developed artistic culture and who are the shortest people in the world. I think they made The Bradshaws.

But no matter who made them, I really loved the idea of a culture who celebrated their shadows.

So, as the sun set further and my shadow stretched 30 feet in front of me, I experimented with what it can do. I walked closer to the high, smooth rock-face where I could send my shadow right up to the top. The rock became a movie screen and if I leapt into the air, my shadow became detached from my body and flew across it. I could make my shadow fly! The shadows were so releasing, they made us laugh and we felt like we were full of magic by just watching them.

I think the painting was in that particular place because of the high, flat, rock-face nearby. Whatever the reason, it was certainly saying: "There's a good place round here to fly your shadow".

With this experience my confidence grew. I realised that every day, in everything we do, there is a richer, more magical world right beside us and that we are much closer to this magical world than we realise, all we have to do to find it, is to think in a different way.

What separates us from the people who made these joyful paintings, isn't time, it's a belief. A belief that in the natural world there is everything we need in order for all of us to have the highest quality of life we can ever have. It leads to a life where everyone can make their shadows fly.

2

A long way down the Gibb River road, I finally saw some Aboriginal women sitting by the side of the road at a truck stop. I stopped the land-cruiser and got out. I went over to them and said hello and I asked if I could go hunting bush tucker with them.

Without getting up, one of them said "What d'you wanna do thet for?"

I couldn't believe it, I'd come half-way round the world to go hunting with the Aborigines and they didn't want to go.

I just stood there, feeling stupid but this was too important to me to let go of and so I tried again and said that I *really* wanted to do this.

Time went by. Flies buzzed. The women had that completely uninterested look on their faces which seemed to say they didn't give a damn about the present. In fact, they were very much in the present. I waited, because I didn't know what else to do. One of them, the youngest girl, got up at last and said that she knew of a woman who gathered bush tucker and she would go and ask her if she'd take me with her.

Time went by and I wished I knew how to wait so that it passed quickly. She came back and asked me to follow her. We walked through the bush, littered with plastic bags to a flyblown dump that is an Aboriginal reserve camp. The girl introduced me to Reila, one of the elder women. I felt, straight away, that I was in the presence of someone who knew all about the meaning of life and everything in it. Reila agreed to be my teacher, my "auntie".

She took me hunting many times. She didn't belong to this part of the country, her family had been given sugar by missionaries who used it to lure them out of the desert into ring fenced reserves where they were given more sugar until they were addicted and then converted to Christianity. They suffer terribly from diabetes.

But the Aborigines whose land this was, were very good to Reila's family and they showed them what there was to hunt in the area. Reila didn't eat the sugar and she took her mattress outside and slept under the stars every night. She gathered wild food every day and when she got home with a full cooliman (basket), the men would always be asking her for some. She never gave them any, she told them if they wanted bush tucker, they had to go out and get it themselves.

The men were drunk. I asked her about that but all she would say was that was "men's business."

There was a fully stocked shop on the reserve and the Aborigines had all the money they needed from the mineral rights from mining companies so they could buy whatever food they liked. Yet Reila went out into the searing heat every day to gather wild food. I asked her why she did it.

She said "For the flavour."

Of all the adventures we had together, the day that I had the biggest realisation about the quality of this life and what it lead to, was the day we went hunting goanna, a family sized lizard. About five of us went: Reila and another woman everyone called Auntie Nada, the young girl whose name was Lucy and a two year old boy called Trent who had been left with them by his mother.

I didn't take Tony with me on this trip because I had noticed that the women behaved differently when he was around – they always sang

Jesus songs before we ate and I had a feeling they were only doing that because he was there. I wanted to know what they did when he wasn't there.

We would have to drive a long way to get near the goanna hunting ground. At dawn, I went to collect Reila and found her drinking water. She had explained that Aborigines don't drink during the day, they fill up before they go out so they are fully hydrated and then they drink again at dusk. I did the same.

When we got there, she told me to park in the shade of the only tree. Lucy and Trent stayed there, under the tree. This was Day Camp. Reila, Auntie Nada and I headed out into the bush. The heat built up around us as we walked.

We were looking for tiny signs in the dusty earth where the goanna had burrowed. The women held their hands clasped behind their backs so I did this too and without the distraction of my hands, my eyesight improved. Hour after hour went by and though we found many goanna holes, all of them were empty. There was no sign of giving up, we couldn't go back to the Day Camp with empty hands. We were staying out there until we found some food.

When I had asked Reila to show me what a goanna looks like in one of my books, she kept pointing to the different animals saying "Ah! *Flavour*!" She said there used to be a lot of animals in the bush but they are all gone now. I asked her if it was to do with the cattle stations but she just said that when the white people leave Australia, she thinks the animals will come back.

The first white man her family had ever seen was in the time of her grandfather. He had been out walking by a waterhole in the desert when he saw the man. They killed each other.

She told me about an Aboriginal freedom fighter called Pigeon who had set fire to every new police station as it was built and then disappeared into the bush and no matter how many men they sent after him, they could never find him. It was as though he had simply flown away.

Reila said "If that Pigeon had won the war, this would be a free country now."

*

Finally, we found a goanna.

Then came the long, long walk back to the Day Camp and the hunger was coming in waves and the misery was setting in as I thought about how we'd now have to skin this horrible thing and deal with its head and its guts and the flies it would attract and I just thought I'm really not cut out for this, the reality is much, much harder than I thought. I've got it all wrong.

And I did have it all wrong because when we finally got back to the others sitting under the tree, Reila handed over the goanna to Lucy and told me that we hunters were now going to sleep. The relief of this offer of sleep while someone else cooked us a meal was absolute bliss. This is how it's *always* done.

From the moment we left, Lucy had set about collecting fire wood. All day she kept watch for us to cross the horizon and when we did, she lit the fire. By the time we reached her, the fire was a perfect bed of embers ready for a BBQ.

I'm not sure if she gutted the goanna before putting the whole thing on the embers because by that time I was asleep.

There is nothing more comforting than to be woken after a long hunt by the sweet delicious smell of roasted meat. The goanna was ready. We hunters sat up, got comfortable in the cool, breezy shade and were handed chunks of the most satisfying meat I have ever tasted. Reila explained how the fat was very light and transparent not like the thick yellow fat of cattle. She said that wild food was very rich, you don't need much to fill you up. And she was right. Soon, the tiredness had left me, the hunger had left me and the meat seemed to be the very thing I needed in order to replenish what I had spent in getting it.

And then I realised I was *more* than replenished; I felt a lightness of spirit, but more mature this time than how I'd felt when we'd first set out. And I realised that all I wanted was to get up now and go hunting again. Which is good because that's exactly what we needed to do.

It might have been at this meal that I asked Reila about the turtle drawings. It had been difficult to ask about it because whenever we'd got to the parts in my book that mentioned sacred things, the women would just shut down and refuse to engage with me about it at all. Which I can understand now, these are very special and private things and have no business being on display to people who haven't been through the challenge of getting there themselves to have earned the right and the ability to see them.

But on this occasion, perhaps because I had been the one who had found the goanna, they had allowed me to see something special when they had killed it. I came to realise that it is only in the act of hunting and gathering that understanding of the bigger picture is revealed. It's Nature's contract with every living thing: do the job you are designed to do and you will be rewarded with answers to what you are curious about. It's a perfect contract. Wild foods are in need of our services to spread the seeds and quickly kill the weak in a herd, and as we do the jobs, Nature rewards us with insights.

You can't explain to someone else what's been revealed to you because you know it with your whole being, not just with words. This ensures that Nature has a relationship with you personally, nobody can get in between, and everyone who wants to know the answers must do the work to get them.

But, I *can* tell you what Reila told me about the turtle drawings. I'd asked her if they were the spirits of the animals and she had laughed at me and said that white people always think like that but no, they weren't the spirits of the animals.

She explained that at the time of her grandfather they had all lived in the Aboriginal way in the desert. Their family of 12-15 people would camp for a few days by a water hole and hunt in the area. Then they'd walk on across the desert to the next water hole and hunt there for a few days and so on round the desert throughout the year. When they'd get to a water hole they hadn't been to for a while, they couldn't always remember what there was to hunt in the area so they'd look on the rock walls for the etchings and that was their menu.

I thought back to the place of the turtle drawings. It made perfect sense. I thought of the family who must have made their camp there, of the fun the children must have had splashing about in the fresh deep pool beside the smooth flat rock in the blazing sun, the hunters coming back with a sea turtle to BBQ. How the hunters would have slept in the shade as the others had cooked it in it's shell and they'd have woken up and feasted on the oily and delicious meat, so satisfying to have the energy spent replenished. And within that feeling is a deep sense of contentment and understanding and belonging. Pure heaven. I can tell you the words but I can't do it in a way that you can feel the satisfaction, or understand the depth of what there is to know because you have to do it yourself. All I can say is that the rewards are ten times greater than the effort and a thousand times better than anything I've experienced in the modern world.

Every etching on that rock wall says "There are turtles to eat here!", every etching a tally to make sure that not too many are taken and so there are always turtles to eat. The Aborigines were so advanced as people that we whites just couldn't understand them.

On the way back from the goanna hunt everyone had fallen asleep in the back of the land-cruiser, everyone using everyone else as a pillow. They were so relaxed in each others company and so accepted and they so deeply belonged together. I realised that no matter how much I wanted to be, I am not an Australian Aborigine, no matter how long I stayed or how much I learned, I would never be one of them.

I realised though, that we must have had hunter-gatherers in Britain too. I wondered what could possibly have happened to turn us away from this wonderful life where we had all eaten such rich and delicious food, where we had all been completely free, living in the best places and where we all had jobs which were important and which brought us rich and deep understanding of something real and precious, every day in everything we did. How could we possibly have left it? For a life like this?

The next day I told Reila that I loved the Aboriginal way better than the western way.

She said, "I know."

I returned to Britain to learn the wild food of my own country and to find out what had happened to us to turn us away from the life we had loved so much.

Learning How to Think Like a Hunter-Gatherer

Part 2

How we Separated from Nature

1

When I got back to Britain, life got in the way for a while and I felt very lost without the Aboriginal way of life around me.

But when I heard about an ancient standing stone not far from where I went to live in the Welsh hills, it brought me back to my journey.

Nobody knew what this stone was all about and so I thought I might find it and see if I could work out what it was for. Even though hunter-gatherers don't put up stone monuments, they don't have to, they have everything anyone could ever need without hauling great stones about the countryside, but at least it was a mystery from our past and might shed some light on what had happened back then, to separate us from Nature.

I found the stone because it made me jump. I'd seen it out of the corner of my eye and I'd thought it was a person, a very tall person standing there. I certainly hadn't liked the fright it gave me.

After that, I noticed the same shape of that standing stone in the local church: it was the shape of the front door; the shape of the windows; the shape of the light cast across the floor; and, as a much smaller version, it was the shape of the gravestones. I felt it wasn't a coincidence that I'd thought it was a tall person out of the corner of my eye and it reminded me of the methods used by Mobutu, former President of Zaire (the old Belgium Congo) to make his presence felt when he was thousands of miles away in the capital. It felt like someone much bigger than me was watching me. Which of course is what they want you to think in church too, they want you to think that God is watching you and, by extension, His clergymen. I made a mental note about these single standing stones and moved on to another mystery that someone told me about in passing.

Newgrange, a monument in Ireland that is older than Stonehenge and still intact. I was amazed that I'd never heard of it. It's a massive man-made mound on the top of a hill with a long passage built inside it which leads to a chamber. At the Midwinter Solstice, the sun rises on the far horizon and sends a shaft of light down the passage which illuminates the chamber. It is still in perfect alignment to this day. I was interested to learn more so, at the first opportunity I flew to Dublin, hired a car and drove north to the Boyne valley. I spent the night in a nearby hotel and set off early the next morning to visit it.

When I caught my first sight of the dome from the tour bus I thought it had been white-washed. In fact the whole thing looked like a 1970's idea of a flying saucer. But, it wasn't. It wasn't white-wash either but squares of white *quartz* and each piece had been put back where the archaeologists had worked out it belonged by the trajectory it had made to its resting place on the ground.

Almost blocking the entranceway is a massive stone, covered with rock art. The etchings are deep in the granite and depict three spirals, they call it the Tri-spiral and there are lots of theories about what they might mean, but nobody knows for sure.

I wanted to work out what it was all about and so I kept concentrating on exactly what I was experiencing as we bowed our heads and entered the cool, musty passage, walking slightly uphill and for longer than you'd think, until we were standing upright in the chamber.

In there, there were three enclaves. In one of them was a large stone bowl in which they had found plant seeds, on the other side there was one which had held animal bones and in the enclave in the middle, taking pride of place, they had found the remains of humans.

The guide turned out the light and it was pitch black. A re-enactment of the Midwinter Solstice sunbeam began. It slowly illuminated the chamber, reached the furthest enclave where the human remains were found, stayed there for a few minutes then retreated, leaving us in total darkness once more.

The guide had been lucky enough to stand there during the real thing (it's done by lottery) and she said that it was so much better than the electric light because the sunbeam seemed to be alive and exploring it's way along the ground and when it reached the chamber, it filled it with such warmth, it seemed to fill up the whole of your inside too

All the while I kept my focus on what I was *actually* experiencing rather than letting my mind run on to what it all meant. That would come later, now I was gathering.

We walked back down the passageway and out into the sunshine and then I did the tour again.

The most striking thing on that first day, apart from the sight of it all, was the *sound* of the tour guides' voice when she told us how amazing the light had looked in real life, how it had looked like it was *alive*, how it had flooded the chamber with such *warmth* and how it had left the chamber in darkness for another year. There was magic in her voice. So, I decided to follow that magic and concentrate on the sunbeam.

As I went back to the hotel, I mulled over the sequence of events. I had a feeling they were very familiar but I couldn't quite put my finger on it, so I just kept running the sequence over and over in my mind as I went down and had a meal, and before I went to sleep: a shaft of sunlight is directed into a passage that runs deep into a mound and illuminates a chamber, retreats, then does it again the next morning for several mornings, then leaves it in darkness for another year.

By the morning, I felt I had a good idea of what was going on at Newgrange and so I went back to check my hunch by looking at the anatomy of the mound and this is what I think is happening there: the three spirals on the entrance stone relate to the three enclaves in the chamber at the end of the passage: the plant seeds, the farmed animals and the people. The mound itself is where the sun is being directed to make love to Mother Earth.

*

I felt very encouraged by the visit to Newgrange and remembered that Stonehenge has a Summer Solstice alignment and so, at the first opportunity, I went to visit it. I thought it might be the same kind of thing as Newgrange but actually it is quite different in structure so I knew I would have to begin from scratch.

The first thing that struck me as I walked along the tunnel under the road looking at the drawings of how it was built, was that it had taken such a huge amount of effort over 12 generations to build it and yet we can't remember what it's for.

I sat down and breathed the sweet, fresh air and listened to the skylarks. Those skylarks' ancestors had been singing up there when this was built. I looked at the clouds, they had been there when this had been built too. Though I couldn't get in to explore amongst the stones as I had done as a child, all I could do was to think about the common ground between the people who had built it and me because I knew that we have not changed, our needs are still the same.

It had taken 12 generations to build so 12 generations of families had lived within walking distance of this building site.

How We Separated from Nature

As a woman, I would have had my own cooking fire. At the end of each day, my husband and children would have come home in need of food and comfort and love. People cannot live without love. So, for at least 12 generations, the henge works were surrounded by the stars of these cooking fires each one with a woman beside it, radiating love.

The monument itself didn't seem to be radiating love.

The trees on Salisbury Plain were all cut down so that the horizon could be clear in order to note the sun and moon rising points and I wondered what the women would have said about that? About the loss of the beautiful trees and magical places they made. Would they have said anything about the loss of the great umbrella against the rain above them? Would they have minded the land flattened to make a road for the approaching stones? Did some of them just go along with it and did some of them stand in the way? How bad did it get? What were they appeased with or restricted by?

A settlement where people remained all year round and without the tree canopy shelter must have become very muddy. And because they needed to see the horizons, the man-made shelters would have had to be down in the dips. In the Winter, when cold air sinks, that mud would have frozen. An awful place to live which strangely describes what people often think of as being the conditions of hunter-gatherers. But only fools live like that.

Then I thought about the men. How big and strong they were to be able to haul those stones, make roads for those stones, dig holes for them, shape them and get them into position. Then I thought about how clever they were as well to do all the alignments and star gazing.

But there the image separated from my own experience and I realised it didn't make sense. In my own experience big, strong men are most often not the ones with the greatest intellect. Those men are usually smaller - not always of course, but mostly. So, I realised that beside every stone, at every stage of the way where decisions had to be made, there was a smaller man telling a bigger man what to do. And the more the men hauled the stones, the bigger they became and the less physical work the smaller men did, the smaller they became. The class system of blue collar workers and white collar works was born.

At the end of the day, no doubt the smaller men gathered round the fire to discuss the day's progress and to make plans for the next day. I'm sure they didn't sit with the big men who were unwinding, probably fairly loudly, with their families at their own fires. The noise of their congratulations or commiserations probably made the small men move their fires further away so they could think. And they probably moved them up the hill and inside the henge so they could see the horizon better. It made them feel superior to the others.

No doubt the small men's children had to keep quiet in the evening. I expect they looked at the children of the big men being tossed high into the air and wished their own fathers could do that.

The women of the small men probably had other women to do their work for them. And so they became smaller. It must have made the daily work of ordinary women much harder, despite their constant laughter and singing, because now some of them were simply spending their whole day making themselves look pretty. It must have lead to upsets that had never happened before.

Building this unnatural thing had produced divisions between people on all levels – physical, mental, social and spiritual. As hunter-gatherers we had shared our knowledge, leaving drawings on the rock walls to tell others what there was to hunt in the area but now we have this monument being built, we have some people knowing the bigger picture of the plans and some people not knowing anything at all. "Divide and rule" is the phrase that springs to mind.

I realised, at this point, that I needed to find out about the Druids because they have an association with Stonehenge today. Though I hadn't yet got to the heart of what Stonehenge was all about, I had a line of enquiry to follow which would help me so I went home to follow it.

I didn't return to Stonehenge for many years but when I did I had all the pieces I needed to understand it. For now though, I was to follow a more cerebral journey in search of one of the crucial pieces I needed. Though it meant I wasn't visiting sites but piecing together human nature with historical events, I found my way none the less and it all began to unfold and reveal what had really happened to separate us from Nature.

2

I wanted to know what a Druid is and what a Druid really does. I picked up a few books but I didn't find what I was looking for so I started casting about in my mind for anything I already knew about Druids. Fragments that are still in our culture today are like little pieces of pottery found in archaeological sites, they lead to information. I thought of the phrase "all fire and brimstone" because it has a connection to wizards and druids. It certainly felt like there was forgotten knowledge around that phrase because it seemed to be referring to an event that we all knew about, but what could it be?

What is "brimstone" anyway? I looked it up in the library and found out that it's the old word for *sulphur*. What do people need fire and sulphur for? I looked that up and found something very interesting indeed. Fire and sulphur are what you need in order to extract iron from iron-ore.

So, the Druids were smelting iron.

I did some research about the Iron Age and where it came from and found that it originated at the head waters of the Danube where this process was first invented. This was the land of the Celts. So the Celts brought the Iron Age to Britain and the rest of Europe. It all made sense that the Druids lead the Celts because the Druids developed the technology of how to get iron out of iron-ore and the Celts fashioned it into iron tools.

But this was so much later than Stonehenge so the Druids didn't have anything to do with Stonehenge when it was built. However, rather than going back to Stonehenge at this point, I decided to continue looking at how the Iron Age was spread because in there would be the answer to why we had laid down stone tools and picked up iron tools which was a key moment of our separation from Nature. What was going through our *heads* at that time?

As always I looked to today to see how it is done now then looked back with this information in mind to see if it would make sense. I realised that when new technology enters our lives today it isn't just one person who goes out into the world and shows everyone how to use the new thing, it's a brand and people get training and then go out to a new territory, set up a demonstration and get people to buy it.

So, I thought about the Druids getting their training at the head waters of the Danube and then setting off in search of virgin territory and setting up a demonstration. To protect their livelihood, the Druids didn't have patents but they could stop people from trying this at home by making it look like magic.

Fire is always more magical at night and so I imagined they would send out word to all the farming settlements around to come and watch the show one clear and moonlit night.

Druids wear robes these days, so I'm sure they wore them then and it had the same effect, making us think they know something that is somehow beyond our ken – interesting that when men wear long skirts we think of them as being super intelligent and in possession of magical powers.

The Druids would no doubt have circled the fire making sure it wasn't catching the grass anywhere but the effect was mesmerizing: be-robed figures circling the flames as they grew higher. Then there was the moment when sulphur was added to the fire and it caused great clouds of yellow smoke to appear around the circling figures who pulled up their hoods against the chemical. As they loaded the iron-ore into the fire, they no doubt spoke to each other, getting the mix right and it must have sounded like they were chanting strange words - they were foreigners after all. No doubt drums beat out an ever quickening rhythm to heighten the tension until finally, with lighted torches held high for all to see, they moved round to where there was a stone laid on the ground with a deep groove cut into it and waited..........for the first trickle of molten iron to appear. What colour is molten iron at this point? Blood red. The blood of the stone.

When the onlookers realised what was happening there were no doubt objections: "You've got no right to take the blood out of that stone!"

And the Druids stood up with hands held aloft and spoke the words of their most famous bard, Taliesin, saying: "*I* am the rage in a bull, *I* am the fight in a blue salmon, *I* am the might in a storm and so *by the powers vested in me*, I have the *right* to take this blood out of this stone."

And if you still didn't agree with them after hearing that and wanted to put a stop to this, they were the ones with the swords after all.

*

This led me to thinking about King Arthur.

King Arthur lived much later just after the fall of Rome, when England was about to be invaded by all and sundry and so it needed defending. The call went out for: "Whoever can pull the sword out of the stone will be the next King of England." I realised they didn't mean "Whoever can pull this sword that's sticking up out of this stone", they meant "Whoever can get iron out of iron-ore to make swords and so defend England will be the next King."

And why would Arthur have been able to do this as opposed to anyone else? Because Arthur's teacher was Merlin, and Merlin was an old Druid. It makes sense too that Excalibur was found in the lake because the Celts, all those years before, had thrown beautiful iron items into the lakes and rivers to give thanks for where they had first worked out the technology at the head waters of the Danube.

*

Going back to how the Iron Age was spread across Britain. I wanted to know what went through our *heads* at the point that we converted to iron because it was a key moment of separation from the Stone Age. So, again I looked at what happens now because we have not changed. I looked at how every new technology is sold to us today and by carefully watching every advert on television, reading every advert in a range of different magazines and noticing every billboard, I realised that when we are sold something new three distinct stages occur in our thinking.

First, the advertiser sows a seed of doubt in our minds about what we are using right now because he can't sell something to someone who is happy with what they have, so he has to make them unhappy with it. For example: "Whites not white enough?" You may never have thought your whites weren't white enough, but now you're wondering.

Next, the advertiser presents the solution to the problem he has created: "Use new Dazzle Automatic, it'll make your whites white!" Phew! And you're happy again.

Third, you are told there's a time limit "It's only on special offer till the end of the week."

And so, within less than two minutes, you have lost faith in what you're using and are rushing out to buy the new thing.

I looked at dozens of adverts from new outdoor clothing materials, to computer technology, to gym membership and they all follow this three stage structure. So, if it happens now and it works, why think it only began this century. It's got to be the same at every stage of our history because our needs have always been the same. So I juxtaposed this strategy onto the way the Iron Age was spread through Britain to see if it made sense.

From that demonstration, the iron axes were then smelted and when they were ready, salesmen would take one and head out to the outlying areas, no doubt listening for the sounds of chopping. Being Celts, they were dark, they were strangers and they were no doubt handsome because we are more likely to trust people if they are handsome.

Enter the dark, handsome stranger into the woodland clearing where men are chopping up a tree with their flint axes. In his hands is something new and shiny. And he says: "Stone axe taking you *all day* to chop up that tree?" The seed of doubt is sown. The men look down at their flint axe and instead of marvelling at them as they always have since they were tiny children watching their father and grandfather, they now see them as being rather slow.

The stranger presents his bright shiny, extremely sharp iron axe and slices it into the wood, saying in a sing-song sort of voice that gets into your head whenever you're swinging your stone axe. "I can do that job in *half* the time!" When the seed of doubt is sown, you can't ever go back. The doubt breaks your belief in what you are using so that you will never pick it up again and believe in it as you once did. It's instant. The seed of doubt is the greatest weapon of mass destruction ever invented. It can turn you against anything you believe in, within seconds.

The Iron Axe salesman says they'd better hurry to get one, before all their neighbours do, or there won't be any dead wood left to chop up.

But *how* do they get one of these iron axes?

The salesman only wants one thing: chopped wood delivered up to the smelting place on the top of the hill. The woodcutters only want one thing: an iron axe. So, for every load of wood they take to the top of the hill, they are given a small piece of iron in return. Collect these small pieces of iron together and when you've got enough, take them to the iron worker and he will melt them into an iron axe.

No doubt there were disputes about the weight of these little pieces of iron and so a standard weight was set using a set of scales and a stone and as proof of their validity, the Druids mark was pressed into them.

And so working for someone in exchange for little bits of metal came into our lives.

3

Thinking about the method of converting people to iron, I realised I had seen the same thing happen to convert people to Christianity. While I was walking across the Arizona desert, I'd heard about a group of missionaries who were converting the Indians. Ironic really, when you know the other story about why they were called Indians. Apparently, when the first Spanish explorers came across them they called them "Un gente que viva in Dios" – "A people who live in God." *In Dios*, In God, *Indians*. I had wanted to know what they were saying to make them believe they are superior to Nature and therefore convincing them they have the right to pen in animals for their own convenience. In other words, converting the spirit of hunter-gatherers into farmers.

So, for two days I had walked through this Indian reservation trying to find the missionaries. They saw me coming, a young white woman pushing a pram (containing my camping kit and a guard dog), and invited me in with open arms.

The Indians were in a very poor state on this reservation, they didn't have any work or much in the way of medical facilities or schools. They had nothing to live for, they clearly hadn't found anything in the western way of life worth-while and because they couldn't have their own way of life anymore, they drank. The missionaries were well fed, lived in an air-conditioned mobile home and had all the trappings that are destroying the world.

First, they got a group of the most wretched Indians together, sat them down and gave them sugary coffee. Then they brought in an Indian who had already converted. He was well fed and wore smart new clothes.

The first thing he said to them was "Do you realise that you're sinning?" and he sowed the seed of doubt.

He explained that if they didn't do something about this sin they would go to an even worse place when they died and would remain there for all eternity.

But, there was one way they could rid themselves of all this sin and be clean before they died, and he presented the solution: all they had to do was to bow down and accept Jesus Christ as their Lord and Master.

And then came the time limit: they had to do it quickly because if they didn't do it before they died, they would go straight to Hell and since nobody knows when they are going to die, they needed to do it *right now*.

He added that if they did do it right now, the missionaries would give them a good meal, provide medicine and set up a co-operative to get them work. After supper, I found out that the missionaries had to reach a monthly target of conversions in order to keep their mobile home.

Did the Indians convert? I don't know, all I do know is that whenever white men were around the Aboriginal reserve in Australia, Reila had sung Jesus songs after every meal.

*

It's interesting that when Christianity was brought to Britain we were so fiercely against bowing down to accept Jesus Christ as our Lord and Master, that we were slaughtered in our tens of thousands. Ours was the bloodiest conversion of any country in Europe.

*

So, if you can apply this three stage sales technique to anywhere in the history of progress and development, where did it all begin? Where did the very first seed of doubt come from and what was it?

Again, I looked through my mind for fragments of information in the great archaeological site that is our common cultural knowledge. And I realised that right under my nose there was in fact, a whole story about how and why we were separated from Nature. In Genesis of course.

I got out a Bible and had a good read of the Adam and Eve story to see if I could make any sense of it. What struck me very quickly was how different this story was compared to the one I was expecting to read. I thought I was going to read about how we became farmers because God made us superior to the animals and how He gave us the right to pen them in for our own convenience and in return we were to be good stewards of the land, because that's what I'd been told so many times when I was walking through the Bible belt in America.

However, what it actually says is that when we took the apple from the Tree of Knowledge, God *punished* us by making us farmers. He said that if we wanted to have the knowledge of God, we now had to do all the work that He had to do. When we had lived in the Garden of Eden, we were hunter-gatherers and God had provided us with all our food but now that we had disobeyed Him, we had to do all the tilling of the soil, the sowing of seeds, the watering of plants and so on.

Farming is explained as being a punishment for wrong doing, not as being our right because we are superior. And farming really is punishment. If you've ever farmed or gardened, you'll know how much hard work it is compared to just going out and gathering what looks nice without having had to do any of the hard work to make it grow.

It took me another *13 years* to figure out the next bit.

How We Separated from Nature

By this time I had learned the edible plants here in Britain and I was hunting and gathering wild food every day, providing at least 80% of my family's daily food. Every time I stepped outside my door, my sense of wonder grew because now I was being provided for by Nature and every day I would come home with a full basket.

The world and everything in it had become so beautiful to me in ways I had never seen before and often all I could do was just to stand there letting it flood through me, filling me up with wonder as though I was physically drinking in the magic around me and I'd find that tears of joy would be falling from my eyes at the sheer amazement of it all.

And then I noticed that every time I saw something beautiful, I would feel a lump gather in my throat. It was not like the lump of sadness. Instead of making everything taste tinny and loading my eyes with tears, this lump was allowing everything to come down my throat and as it did so and I swallowed, it massaged the *inside* of my neck against my backbone. The more I abandoned myself to the beauty I was drinking in, the stronger the massage and it felt like I was in absolute *heaven*. If I relaxed at this point, the feeling would go so deeply within my body, pushing on through my arms and legs and down into my feet, pushing away the debris and making me a clear conduit for that beauty.

It felt so right and it was being operated by completely abandoning myself to the belief that Nature would always provide for me.

What is this lump, I wondered? I asked other people if they had ever experienced this and I couldn't find a single person who knew what I was talking about. So I'd just have to figure it out myself. And then I realised that the only lump in the neck I'd ever heard of is called the Adam's Apple.

Very interesting.

Very interesting that if we abandon ourselves to the purest belief in Nature, it swells our Adam's Apple so that it presses into our spinal column and massages us into absolute heaven. So, it would make sense then, that if we no longer *believed* that Nature would provide for us, the Adam's Apple wouldn't work.

Why would we suddenly no longer believe that Nature would provide for us when it always had done?

Because along came somebody sowing the very first seed of doubt.

We have in our culture a memory of being so stupid we thought the sun wouldn't rise tomorrow. I wonder how that got there? As hunter-gatherers we had no such fear, the sun had always risen, but when a handsome stranger came along and said "Do you realise the sun might not rise tomorrow?" of course we suddenly thought it might not.

Then the stranger presented the solution. He would make an offering to the sun God on our behalf. This would make sure the sun would rise tomorrow. In order to make this offering, he would need the very best meat, the very best gourd of alcohol and the prettiest maiden and he needed these things before sunset. He would take them into the wilderness on top of the hill away from the people and make the offering for us all through the night.

And it worked! The sun rose the next morning.

All he had done was to sow the seed of doubt, present the solution and give us a time limit. Nobody could doubt him, because they couldn't take the risk that the sun might not rise, even though it always had done.

The man probably continued doing this all around the country whenever he met hunter-gatherers and enjoyed himself very much indeed.

The next man who came along said "Do you realise that Nature might not provide for you?"

No, we'd never even thought about that, but now that you mention it, what can we do?

So the stranger presented the concept of farming. He had learned it somewhere out East. He would stay with us, teaching us how to do it and in return we would build him the best house in the village, give him the best food, make him the best sets of clothes and give him the prettiest woman. For the rest of his life, this man would tell people what to do without having to do a stick of work himself. But for everyone else, life now consisted of digging and sowing and weeding and watering and picking off slugs and feeding animals morning and night and dealing with their foot rot and birthing their babies and there was never a break.

The ultimate aim in life had now changed, too. As a hunter-gatherer, the ultimate status was reached when you knew how to do everything for yourself so that you were completely free. With the coming of farming everyone wanted to be the man who just told others what to do whilst having everything done for him.

Not only was it *a lot* harder to farm than just taking a stick and some friends and going off hunting to get something delicious for supper, it was even harder doing it while someone else didn't do anything at all. But, if you asked those farmers why they didn't just go and hunt for their supper, they'd tell you that Nature might not provide for them, even though this was totally against all their own experiences and all the experiences of all the generations that had ever existed on Earth before them since the beginning of time.

*

And what of the Tree of Knowledge?

That's much closer than you think. Just think of what the Adam's Apple is massaging…it's the trunk of your neck which holds up the dome of your head….which in other words, is the Tree of Knowledge.

I think the Adam and Eve story is absolutely true. The first people to doubt that Nature will provide for us, no longer felt the Adam's Apple exquisitely massaging the inside of their neck because as soon as they stopped believing, the apple didn't swell, it became disengaged, it was "picked".

And the consequence of not believing that Nature will provide for you is that you now *have* to farm. Which is what it says in Genesis, farming is the punishment for not believing that Nature will provide for you. Which makes sense.

In Genesis it also says that because we picked the apple, women would now have painful periods and would suffer in childbirth – which I always thought was very spiteful. So, I looked up more information about the spinal column at the point where the massaging was taking place to see if there was any biological reason for this.

The spinal column in the neck contains the thickest bundle of nerve tissue anywhere in the body and it is encased in tissues which contain hormones. One of these hormones is oestrogen, the hormone which creates sexual passion and desire in women.

So when we were hunter-gatherers and we completely believed that Nature would provide for us, our Adam's Apple was being swelled and was massaging the inside of our spinal column every time we saw something beautiful. At every stroke of that massage, oestrogen was being released into our blood, making us feel deeply sexual and physically passionate.

It would make sense then that if we were no longer getting that oestrogen released into our blood every time we saw something beautiful, our periods *would* be more painful and we *would* suffer more in childbirth. And since it says that it was *Eve* who picked the apple, maybe this swelling and massaging in the neck only happens in women anyway.

Maybe Adam wasn't a person at all, maybe Adam was just the apple...

So, to sum up what I had learned about how we were separated from Nature: it was done by a series of people coming into our lives with something to sell us. But the only way they could make us interested in what they had was to get us to cast doubt on what we were doing or using or believing in already. In this way we were made to be afraid that Nature wouldn't provide for us, even though it always had, and to doubt our own abilities, even though we had always been able to do everything.

Now that I had a good idea of what had happened, I turned my attention to the other thing I had come to learn: how to be a hunter-gatherer in my own country.

Part 3

Becoming a Hunter-Gatherer in Britain

1

From the Welsh hills, I moved to Devon, to the town where I was born. Not because I knew anyone there, but because I'd been so rootless all my life, I wanted to belong somewhere. I realised I'd come to the right place when, not long after I arrived, I noticed an article in the local newspaper about a woman who was taking people out gathering wild food.

Clio Wondrausch became my teacher that Spring. She had learned the wild food from her mother who had learned it from her mother before her and so on. She took me out hunting and gathering and taught me the edible leaves and flowers with which to make a Spring salad.

She showed me how to wash the leaves by holding my willow basket under the tap so that it acts like a colander. The willow needs the water to keep it healthy and when you're finished, you just hang it up to dry and it will not rot.

I wasn't expecting the leaves to be so full of flavour. But these were flaming hot! Wild garlic leaves, mustardy cresses, hot peppery flowers and bitter sweet petals mixed together into a fiery green salad, topped with sweet tasting primroses and pink tipped daisies.

I realised that they all tended to grow in their own patches – the nettles were all together in one part of the landscape, the primroses were always along the bank, the wild garlic in a patch down by the river and so on. Just as I keep all my forks together, all my linen together, all my salt together, I realised that Nature is a housekeeper too. She keeps all the clouds together, all the geese together, all the pine resin together. Why? For the same reason that I do, it makes things easier to find. And since hunting and gathering is all about looking for things, it makes perfect sense that everything has a place. And I realised that the wild animals are hunter-gatherers too and it works just like this for them.

And then I realised that what proceeds finding something, is a picture you get in your mind about what you want and then you find it. What if that's how it works all the time? What if it's actually a function of hunting, that you must have the image in your mind first so that you can find the thing because Nature has the power to can keep the two things together: the picture and the thing. That's how hawks find mice, how birds find worms, how deer find the sweetest grasses, they have a very clear image in their mind about what they want to find when they set out for the day and Nature's Housekeeping Power connects the two. I think this is the practical reason why wishes actually work.

I just kept practising. I went out every day and kept learning. Sometimes I learned by mistake. Like when I ate an Arum Lily leaf thinking it was a Sorrel leaf and my tongue swelled up to twice it's size and I couldn't speak or close my mouth for several hours until it had calmed down. After that, I looked very closely at the differences between the two to make sure I would never make that mistake again.

Though both are arrow shaped, the poisonous Arum Lily leaf has a maze of veins on the back and a deep groove running just inside the front edge. I called this groove "the road to hell".

But once I'd learned what was edible and where it was, I could gather enough wild food to feed my family for the whole day in about 30 minutes. We were eating about 3/4 of our daily food from the wild. With 25-30 different kinds of plants to choose from, the Spring salad provided us with hundreds of times more vitamins and minerals than anything grown by Man.

People were commenting on how well I looked and I certainly began to feel amazing. My skin became clear and younger looking, my hair shone, my eyes were clear and bright and I could happily concentrate without feeling fogged up all the time. I felt like I had found the food of the Gods.

Wild plants contain more goodness than cultivated plants. I realised this is because they are growing where they want to grow. Just as I would give my best if I was doing something I wanted to do rather than if I was forced to do it. And I realised that this is something that people and plants and animals have in common. It's why cultivated plants and cultivated animals only have a fraction of the nutritional value that wild plants have. The nutritional value and the hormones are what makes the taste so that explains why wild food has such flavour. It would also explain why Reila had sighed as she'd pointed to the wild animals and said "Ah! *Flavour*!"

I noticed that by eating wild food every day, twice a day, that I had a lot more energy. It was also much more enjoyable to gather from the hedgerows than to gather from the supermarket shelves and it took the same amount of time anyway. Each morning I'd walk down the lane, swinging my basket. Half an hour later I was back with a full basket of the most delicious and nutritious food on Earth for the whole day. Sometimes I'd walk past people digging their gardens and they'd try to stand up to return my wave and say "Good morning", but the strain on their back was always visible.

Often at this point, people will tell me that it's all very well but we aren't all going to be hunter-gatherers again because there are too many people in the world, not enough wild food and that farming is the only way to feed them.

So, I draw their attention to the fact that farming *isn't* feeding everyone: millions of people are dying every year from malnutrition and not just in countries where there isn't enough food. In the USA, over a third of adults are obese. Obesity is another form of malnutrition because the food they are eating doesn't contain the nutrition they need.

Farming is not feeding people on all the other levels that need to be fed either. In England, the second highest killer of young men is suicide. In Scotland it's the highest killer of young men. In our inner cities 3 out of 4 women are on anti-depressant drugs, these drugs are being given to girls as young as 12. Farming is not sustaining people, they either die from the poor quality of the food, or they kill themselves because this way of life does not give us the happiness we need to keep living, or they just suffer.

Only hunting and gathering provides everyone with all the nourishment we need on every level. Which makes perfect sense: how could a way of life which destroys Nature provide fulfilment?

But, people say, we can't all be hunter-gatherers tomorrow. It's a silly question really, because we won't all be hunter-gatherers tomorrow. Tomorrow it's Friday, or whatever day it is when you're reading this and life will be much as the same as it is today, so there isn't a question to answer.

What I think will happen in the near future is that we will do as we always have done and take the easy way *if we have the choice*. If we don't have the choice we will only do what's right, because that's all that's available. The definition of "progress and development" is simply giving people the choice to abuse Nature for their own ends. Nothing more. Having already granted ourselves the right to abuse Nature to do our jobs for us, *we can't stop*.

The only thing that can stop us is Nature itself. And it's doing it right now in many different ways: by dropping the sperm count in the modern world so that people can't reproduce; by making people so depressed they can't reproduce or they kill themselves; by having a finite amount of resources.

Only when we have no choice but to do the right thing, will we *all* stop. And when we do, we'll find that, far from being the most dreadful experience, we are much happier hunting and gathering wild food all together in a group, than slogging away indoors and alone in the drudgery of a life often without purpose or passion, thinking this must be the best there is because we are living in the first world rather than the third world where people are starving to death.

The vast empty fields of England will grow back to being woods and glades again and we will have food on *many* levels instead of just one: roots, green leaves, berries on the bushes, eggs up in the branches, animals in the Earth and birds up in the trees.

Slowly but surely, Nature is taking away the right to abuse her. This is what is *actually* happening. So often I hear people thinking *they* have to come up with a solution but it's only when Man doesn't rule the world that it actually works. If you want to help, all you have to do is abide by the laws of Nature and eat wild food.

*

But, after two months of gathering wild food that Spring, all the edible plants began to disappear or become too woody to eat. By mid June, there was nothing left. I was distraught! I didn't want to go back to Morrisons and eat cultivated food.

I realised I now faced my biggest challenge as a hunter-gatherer: how to find food when there is *nothing left to eat*?

The thoughts kept me on edge for days, the panic rising that this wonderful food had gone till next year and that it is not possible to be a hunter-gatherer anymore in my own country. I couldn't bear to think like that, I knew that allowing the panic in was like allowing myself to get heat stroke, I needed to keep thinking and to keep thinking like an Aborigine and I knew that somehow I would find wild food to eat.

So, I opened my mind and believed that Nature would take care of me. I let my thoughts take me back to Reila and the things she said because I *knew* that in there somewhere would be the clue that would help me.

Then I remembered a story I'd been told about a squad of Australian soldiers who'd once challenged the Aborigines to a race across the desert to see who was the best at survival. The Aborigines had agreed. Both groups would go on foot, carrying everything they'd need. The soldiers were loaded down with water and food, navigational equipment and camping kit. The Aborigines carried just four sticks: their spear, their woomera (for throwing their spear) and a hand-drill set for making fire.

They set off and guess who won the race? Most people say the Aborigines, but in fact the soldiers did. They arrived first despite being exhausted, dehydrated, sunburnt and barely on speaking terms.

The Aborigines had kept up pretty well until three-quarters of the way into the race when they had given up. One of them had remembered they were quite near a place where some honey would be ready about now and it had lured them away and they were found, several days later, munching on honeycomb in the shade. They weren't tired or dehydrated or sunburnt and they were all getting along very well indeed. When asked to explain themselves, the Aborigines said that eating honeycomb in the shade was a much better way to spend your time than competing in a race across the desert.

So in essence they really were the winners because survival isn't just about doing this for a week, it's about doing it forever and they could have gone on living like this quite happily.

To live forever in a desert with just a few sticks and a group of friends, takes genius.

So now, standing on the river bank in the late Spring in South Devon with nothing to eat and not being a genius, I realised how the Aborigines could direct me to wild food where there was none. The Aborigines were saying that the key to surviving in the wild is to go to where you will be the most happy. And there you will find wild food. For them in the desert it was going into the shade and there they would find honey.

So, I asked myself : where will I feel most comfortable and most happy right now? It was mid June and getting hot and muggy. I cast my mind up to Dartmoor and thought about heading up there but then I remembered a camping trip I'd made once in early Summer and was driven down off the moor after only one night, my face and hands and ankles swollen and on fire from being bitten to death by every insect imaginable. No, I definitely wouldn't be comfortable or happy up there right now.

Then I cast my mind in the other direction and wondered if I might like to be by the sea? The thought of the sea with it's cool breezes, clean blue horizons and soft sand felt like a drink of heavenly bliss.

And that's the feeling I was looking for.

That's what roast goanna in the shade feels like.

So, I went down to the sea and when I got there, I found the beach was simply *teeming* with wild food. Fish, they only come into the shallows in Summer; seaweed, it only grows in the Summer; the ancestors of our garden vegetables all of it lush and *ready to eat right now*!

I can't tell you the joy I felt when I realised I had found my way to wild food by asking myself "where would I be most comfortable and most happy?"

It was as though trumpets were sounding in the Heavens and Reila was standing there with me, glowing and proud of me.

But would this work again? At the end of the Summer, when it started to get cold and damp and I no longer wanted to be there because the seaweed was being broken off and washed up on the shore; the fish were disappearing; the ancestors of our garden vegetables had turned woody or were going to seed and there was nothing left for me to eat.

So, I thought about where I wanted to be for the Winter. I knew from past experiences of walking across a continent in Winter and camping out every night, that the best place to be is up high out of the freezing cold air that sinks in valleys and gullies. Dartmoor is the highest place around here. I knew that when we were hunter-gatherers it was heavily wooded, before we'd cut down all the trees during the Iron Age. The woods would make it warm and out of the wind.

I realised that the shortest distance between the sea and the moor is to follow a river because water will always take the shortest route to the sea. I knew from my adventures along the River Dart, that it has two paths beside it: one down low, the other up high, following the ridge of high land. These paths are used by *all* the animals and because animals are barefoot and don't like getting their feet wet either, they are always dry.

So, at the end of Summer when there was nothing left to eat, I turned away from the sea and headed inland along one of these paths heading for the moor. Within a few feet I found there was now an *abundance* of wild food: it lined the path. The berries of Autumn were ripe and ready to eat and away from the salty sea air they lined the route all the way up to the moor.

Upon reaching the moor, I realised that in Winter the woods would be full of animals like deer and boar who don't want to go down hill where it's colder, either. And I thought about whether I'd like to eat that kind of food in Winter and realised that red meat is the *perfect* food for Winter. We don't want to eat fish and salad in Winter, we want to eat red meat and roots. And I thought about the roots and realised that during the Winter, the plants store all their goodness in their roots.

And so the food that's available in the place we'd most like to be, is the *very* food we most want to eat.

But, I knew, from the Hay system of eating, that the combination of eating protein and carbohydrates at the same meal puts on fat, lowers the metabolism and increases cholesterol. Then I realised how perfect that was for us as hunter-gatherers hibernating for the Winter. We would want our food to slow down our metabolism so that we didn't have to keep rushing around feeding ourselves and we would want it to store fat on us to keep us warm. It was all beginning to make perfect sense.

I realised that I had discovered the route we had taken as hunter-gatherers here in Devon. A route where we fit into Nature and it's cycles, where everything we need is only available where we most want to be and at the time of year when we most want to be there.

2

It was in the Spring of the following year that I came across something even more amazing.

I was thinking about turtles and how they come ashore to lay their eggs at the full moon. *Eggs* and *full moon* felt familiar. So I opened my mind and cast around for what it might connect to. Then I remembered that they come together at Easter.

I looked more closely at Easter and realised it is always set as the first Sunday after the first *full moon* after the Spring Equinox and it's when children go looking for *eggs*.

What if birds lay their eggs at the full moon, just like turtles?

What if the full moon somehow acts as a signal to lay their eggs? I did some research online and found that I was absolutely right. But more than that, the full moon acts as a *hormonal trigger* for them to lay their eggs.

The light of the full moon increases the amount of oestrogen in them (hence the word Easter), which triggers them to lay their eggs. It makes sense that we have our egg hunt then – we go hunting for eggs because we *know* they are going to be there.

I was amazed when I realised I had found my way to this piece of information. It felt so right and so familiar that I continued to think about it to see if there was anything else it connected to.

Of course, in our own menstrual cycle. Every woman knows there's a connection between her periods and the moon and how quickly our cycles will synchronise with each other. But why does it happen? I realised that it happens because the light of the full moon must be increasing our own levels of oestrogen so that we all become fertile at the same time and so we all give birth around the same time too.

And if fertility is triggered by the phases of the moon, then conception and birth must be affected by them too. And if women's cycles and birds' cycles and turtles' cycles are all linked to the phases of the moon, why not the cycles of everything else on the planet?

Looking on the internet for anything I could find about this hormonal link with the phases of the moon lead me to a recent book called Biological Time by an American naturalist writer, Bernard Taylor. I ordered a copy from America, read it and found that I was absolutely right. The amount of lunar light triggers our hormones through *every* stage of our development: from birth, through maturity, finding a mate, procreation and death, and it triggers the hormones *of all the other animals and plants too*.

But even more interesting, Taylor realised that it's not just the phases of the moon by itself that are the triggers, they work *in conjunction* with the phases of the sun. So that it's not just under any full moon that the birds lay their eggs.

Each full moon happens at a different point in the sun's position through the seasons. The birds don't want to be laying their eggs at the full moon around Halloween, obviously, there isn't going to be a rich supply of soft worms in the soft earth for the chicks to feed on.

So, you can see how this system of triggering the hormones at *every* stage of development and in every life form at the right time of year makes sure that every animal, insect, fish, plant and human has exactly the right kind of food in the right kind of conditions at every stage of its development exactly where it wants to be in order to thrive.

It's a whole world co-ordination system.

Looking again at how this might affect our own reproductive cycle to see if there was sense in it, I found out that scientists know that sunlight increases our fertility. The most amount of sunlight you can get is at the Summer Solstice so, if you conceive at the Summer Solstice, nine months later you will give birth at the Spring Equinox. Check that against reality and ask any woman when she would most like to give birth in the year and she'll tell you: in Spring. Ask anyone what they most feel like doing on the beach under a full moon at the Summer Solstice, and you begin to get the picture of how perfectly our desires fit in with the bigger picture of Nature's cycles.

And the wild food available at that time of year contains the very substances we need in our bodies to balance what the sun and moon are doing to us hormonally.

Hormones are heaven when they occur naturally and in balance with everything else, but they are hell if they are interfered with, as I'm sure we are all acutely aware.

And in the rest of our life as hunter-gatherers, if you know what effect the phases of the moon and sun have on every other animal, you can tell where they are going to be, what they are going be doing and when, so that you can find everything you need.

To do this, you need to know which day is the Winter Solstice, the Vernal (Spring) Equinox, the Summer Solstice, the Autumn Equinox and the cross quarter days which are the half-way point between a Solstice and an Equinox and which in fact mark the actual change in the season. Then you note the phases of the moon after it and you'll be able to find whatever you want. As hunter-gatherers, we all knew this and we used it all the time.

How do we know we did? Taylor looked into the cultures of tribal people all over the world and found that they mark the Solstice and Equinox points to this day and they note the lunar phases that happen after them, and, just like Easter, have a festival containing food of that time.

This information tells us exactly when the first salmon will arrive from the sea, when the deer will drop their antlers, when the bison will cross a river on their migration north or south, when the eggs will be there and so on.

Taylor realised that this is quite likely to be the reason why in rock art you often see dots and lines beneath drawings of herds of migrating animals because, just as Reila and her people left information for each other about what there was to hunt in the area, it's telling you that this herd will cross the river nearby two full moons and three nights after the Winter Solstice, for example. And so you can position yourself by the river on that *very* day, and catch the stragglers.

This is the original reason why Pagans (which means the religion of the country folk), mark the Solstices, Equinoxes and cross-quarter days and why they note the phases of the moon. They don't know *why* they do it these days, but they know it's important and contains some magical power. The magical power is in the hormones. Hormones are invisible and they make things happen, or appear or disappear. And isn't that the definition of *magic*?

All the Christian festivals follow these points too, only slightly changed no doubt for reasons of domination and separation from Nature. Christmas is just after the Winter Solstice, Candlemas is on the cross quarter day, Easter is on the full moon after the Spring Equinox, St.John's festival is just before the Summer Solstice, Michaelmas is just after the Autumn Equinox and Martinmas is on the cross quarter day.

You might wonder how easy it was, as hunter-gatherers, to know which day is which. At the Solstice points, the sun rises from the same point for 4 or 5 days in a row (solstice means "sun stands still"), then it goes back the way it came. It doesn't do this at any other time of the year except Midwinter and Midsummer.

At the Equinox day and night are exactly equal and the sun rises due east and sets due west.   At various inhabited cave sites, Taylor noted that there are often marks on the wall by a hole in the ground. He put a stick into one of these holes and noticed that it cast a shadow onto the wall directly on the mark on the day of the Equinox.

*

At this point I remembered the Summer Solstice alignment at Stonehenge and I went back to look at it again. The archaeologists, Professors Hoyle and Hawkins had decoded Stonehenge and worked out that it marks the Solstice and Equinox points and the full moons. But they don't know *why* it does this.

Here's what I think Stonehenge is all about:

As hunter-gatherers we were all using the lunar and solar phases to locate our food and we freely shared this information. But then someone got the idea of sowing a seed of doubt about that too. When you get a tool to do your work for you, two things happen. First, you forget that you can do it yourself and start thinking you can't do it and second, the person who is operating the tool can get something from you in return for what it produces. The salesman easily sows the seed of doubt by saying "I'll put up one of these stone monoliths as a Solstice or Equinox marker so that you don't have to remember which day is which, so that you don't forget." Even though nobody had ever forgotten before, we were now afraid and so we believed him. No doubt he had to be honoured with something every time there was an important day, until nobody could remember how to do it themselves because they always relied on him to do it for them. He became very powerful then because he could tell where everything was going to be and when.

Our whole way of life in the modern world is based on people doing this. It's what separates us from being hunter-gatherers – as hunter-gatherers everyone knows how to do everything for themselves, as modern people some know how to do one thing and charge others for it. It's what has resulted in us using only 10% of our brain now because we have tools and machines and other people to do the rest of our work for us and so we can't remember what the rest of our brain is for. Hunter-gatherers use 100% of their brain and know how to do everything including how to live without destroying the planet.

*

I could see that the site of Stonehenge was chosen because the horizon is completely flat all around the edge. There are no hills on the horizon and so you can see exactly where the sun and moon appear and disappear. Apparently, the blue stones are flecked with bits of white inside, do doubt when they were all polished up they must have looked like stars from the night sky.

The architects worked on the calendar until finally they had the whole thing, even the variations in the moon's cycle round the Earth which change every 19 years and which hunter-gatherers also know about and factor into the changing of their festival days.

But, and I think this is the *crucial* thing about Stonehenge, the one thing that Stonehenge can do that hunter-gatherers *don't need to know*, is that Stonehenge can predict eclipses. Hunter-gatherers don't need to know about eclipses because nothing happens at an eclipse.

I think Stonehenge was the ultimate example of when Man sought to use his knowledge as power over others. After generations of separating himself from his fellows and from Nature (the men who worked it out hadn't been hunting or gathering) and negativity had set in. These men had at that time, the ultimate weapon: they knew exactly when the sun would disappear from the midday sky.

I think that Man became God at Stonehenge. And ruled the Earth and sky.

Pretty heady stuff.

Can that ever be seen as positive?

What is much more likely and in keeping with what we know happens, is that he said to everyone they were in grave danger because tomorrow the sun would disappear in the middle of the day. But, he had the power to make it come back again and so save the world from darkness forever.

The central point of the whole monument is the Altar Stone. I think what was going on at Stonehenge was the use of the Altar Stone for the ultimate act of domination: human sacrifice. And, I have a feeling it wasn't goats they were sacrificing, or even men, or middle aged women, or children, but most likely they were sacrificing very beautiful and very frightened and very young, women. A healthy virgin is the most precious of our people. They are also the ones who laugh at authority the most.

*

What springs to mind straight away is a story about its complete opposite, an example of what life is like when men and women are exactly equal. I heard it when I was with the Pygmies in central Africa. When honey is ready up near the topmost branches of a rainforest tree, a

Pygmy man climbs the tree with a smoking stick to smoke out the bees. He will then grab the honey. The adrenaline must be pumping so massively because any minute now the swarm of bees are going to come to their senses and discover he's stealing their treasure and, he's 150 feet up above the ground. All he can think of is getting as much of that honey as he can and getting out of there.

In this highly charged state of excitement he's unlikely to remember that he must also leave enough honey for the bees. So, to help him remember, standing at the bottom of the tree is a woman. As he reaches for the honey, she calls up to him and reminds him to leave some for the bees.

In this way, the Pygmies understand that a man's physical strength and courage makes sure there is honey for today and a woman's inner strength and courage makes sure there is honey for tomorrow. *Together* they will always have what they need.

But, for the last 4,000 years, men have been taking *more* than their fair share. How could that have happened? The only way to be able to take *all* the honey was to get rid of the woman at the bottom of the tree. But how could he get rid of her whilst still wanting her around to cook his meat and sleep in his bed? The only way to get rid of woman while still having her around was to diminish her. By telling everyone she was stupid they stopped listening to her.

Is that what's happened in our culture? Yes. Women have been told they are stupid and have not been listened to since.........when? No idea. Since longer than anyone can remember. There isn't even a date on it because it started before time was kept. We were considered so stupid we weren't even allowed to vote until the last century and so in reality, it kept us out of the way so that men could break *all* the natural laws and take more than his fair share of *everything*. Which is what has happened.

Without women, he could refuse to put back the part that would grow again and take things that weren't meant for him – like taking the animals' freedom for his own convenience, removing their male protectors, keeping them in the ultra-hormonal state of being in milk so that he could take away their babies and eat them as well as drinking their babies' food. It rather describes a monster than a civilised person. It also meant that he and his family who drank the milk would never themselves reach maturity, because you can't reach maturity without being weaned.

With Man free of Woman, he could be really childish and break all the laws of Nature and rule the world. And that's what has happened in the western world. It has been perfectly acceptable to call women stupid, to *sacrifice* them so that some greedy men can live without doing any work except telling people what to do, whilst thinking they are greatly admired, and having the best of everything brought to them for their own pleasure without a care for the consequences.

*

I don't believe that Stonehenge fell over. The stones which have fallen or been dragged away from the site at great personal effort never to be found again, are the most important stones needed to make it work. What are the chances of that happening accidently? Two of the fallen stones are lying directly on top of the Altar Stone. What are the chances of *that* happening accidently?

I think that someone very brave saw through the con and got enough people together to push it over so that it couldn't be used again.

When people are told the folktales about how the stones were put there by the Devil, they laugh at how backward we were to believe in such silly things. The patron saint of England slew a dragon and rescued a sacraficial virgin. They probably think that's silly too. But there's power in that story and where there is power there is something important waiting to be revealed. Here's what I think happened.

So we have the *virgin* that George went to rescue, but where is the *dragon*?

In order to predict an eclipse you have to know where and when the moon will cross the path of the sun, these crossing points are called *nodes*. Total eclipses of the sun only happen when a new moon crosses the sun's path exactly on a node.

In his book SUN, MOON & EARTH, Robin Heath, Honorary Research Fellow of the Dept of Archaeology and Anthropology at the University of Wales, says that:

"To the ancients, the nodes were thought of as the head and tail of a huge celestial *dragon* which was said to have swallowed the sun during an eclipse."

The head of this dragon is called the Caput Draconis.

I think that George slew our of *fear* of the Caput Draconis. So he didn't just rescue the girl, he rescued all of us from the tyranny of the those who had kept us in fear of absolutely nothing in order to enrich their lives with pleasure. In our thanks we bestowed upon him our highest honour.

Did anyone else make a patron saint of a man who had anything to do with dragons or the like? St.Patrick was said to have driven out the *serpents* from Ireland. I'm sure it wasn't snakes at all, but the tyranny of the Caput Draconis

Perhaps, next time there is an eclipse of the sun, flowers can be laid at Stonehenge…

*

In the wrong hands, the knowledge of how to use the sun and moon to locate everything you need led to divisions between people and the sacrificing of women so that some men could pretend to be God.

But in the right hands, this special knowledge shows how the whole of our beings fit perfectly into Nature. It explains why we feel as we do at different times of the year and it reveals the slot that's there for us within all of Nature's cycles. It's where we are needed by Nature and where we are rewarded.

Fragments of this path have been scattered throughout the furthest reaches of our culture over the last 4,000 years, often obscured just slightly so that we can't make sense of it to find our way back. I found this knowledge and the path that makes it work, piece by piece over a number of years by being aware of what I was *actually* experiencing, not what I was *told* I was experiencing. And every time I found another piece, I was reminded how obvious it all really is.

When we follow this path through the year we are taking our rightful place amongst the other animals. We are doing the jobs in Nature that Nature needs us to do, we are taking no more than we need and in return we are rewarded with pleasures and with revelations to make sense of who made us and why we are here and what is the meaning of life. On this path you and your children can live forever.

Here, for the first time in perhaps 4,000 years, is the whole of The Ring of the Wild Food Year brought together in as much of an entirety as I know at this point.

This is the way, the truth and the light; both solar *and* lunar.

PART 4

The Ring of the Wild Food Year

The Ring of the Wild Food Year

*

We are in our cave and the animals are disappearing to have their young. But, just as we are completely losing our meat supply, the edible leaves of Spring begin to emerge.

These fiery plants come up just a few at a time. We add them to the sweet rich roots we roast in the embers and the combination of flavours is a heavenly mix of comfort and fire. As the days go on, we eat more fiery leaves and fewer comforting roots and so we are gradually woken up. As a hunter-gatherer there is no choice but to do the right thing. No choice means there's no inner conflict and so everyone looks and feels gorgeous without even trying.

The Spring weather becomes a mighty turmoil of hot sunshine one minute, sudden hail the next, still hours of warmth and bright sunshine then plunging into dark shadow with great gusts of freezing wind. This combination stimulates all the plants to wake up too. Some need cold to grow and thrive, some need sunshine and warmth. In these dramatic changes, every plant is given the stimuli it needs. The weather is like Nature's contractions as everything is being born.

The leaves and flowers of Spring are the hottest foods of the wild food year and there's no way you can go back to sleep after eating a meal of them. They thin down the blood making it easier to pump around the body after a Winter of piling on the fat. They strip the body of cholesterol. They raise the metabolism so that we can use the energy from our food now instead of automatically storing it. They clean the blood and all the

organs. They even clean the lymph system. The lymph is our body's system of rivers which carries away debris but doesn't have a pump of its own. The only way to get the lymph moving is by physical exercise and after a Winter of hibernating when little exercise was taken, Cleavers have a job to do to get the system cleaned out.

Cleavers actually look like the perfect implement you'd use if you were to clean a system of pipes – like a chimney sweeper's brush. It's taken as a tea. Making a tea out of any plant is simply releasing it's juices. The juices are the hormones. The hormones are the action, the magic.

You experience the hormones as flavours, on a "taste journey". In wild food this journey is very dramatic, for example: Jack-by-the-Hedge tastes sweet to begin with, then the flavours of mustard and garlic start to gather and you feel yourself in for a ride, then they build, expanding on the tongue and getting so strong you feel you're going to burn up and then they suddenly die away leaving a lovely sweet flavour as a lingering after-taste. Each plant has its own taste journey, depending on the hormones that are in them.

The Wild Garlic also has an effect on our skin. After eating some of the first garlic leaves of the year, the skin can prickle with cold spots under the surface which, on the kind of very hot still days that can happen unexpectedly, it will cool the face and arms deliciously. It makes you feel alive. Even though the skin might be getting a little burnt red from the sun, it is cool to the touch. It is as though there is a new layer of skin being stimulated under the outside layer. It feels gorgeous, the perfect combination of warmth from the sun and coolness within.

To gather enough Spring leaves and flowers to feed a family two good meals a day, takes about 20 minutes. For the rest of the day, we make ourselves pretty. The most powerful way of making yourself beautiful from within, is to balance water on your head. With the river running down in the valley and the cave up on the hill, water is needed to be brought up every day. The grace and peace that balancing water on your head produces, relaxes tight muscles down through the spine and tightens up those which have become slack.

Our feet are made of a special kind of tissue that swells with blood when they get cold. Standing on a sun-warmed rock is the most exquisite experience as the warmth penetrates through the feet in the most perfect way.

The skin on our feet is the most absorbent skin on our body. Our feet are designed to absorb moisture and hormones from the plants we are walking across. If mud gets under our toes nails, there are special substances in the rainwater and dew which remove particles so that our toe nails become clean again. The more mud there is, the more moisture there is. Wherever there is muck there is something nearby to clean it with.

Like Spring following Winter.

At the Spring Equinox there is a receptor in our eye which sends this information to the Pineal gland triggering a massive drop off in the production of the hormone melatonin. Melatonin is what has helped us to hibernate for the Winter. But now that it suddenly stops being produced, testosterone levels and oestrogen levels suddenly increase and we feel a great surge of joy, the joy of Spring.

We mark the Spring Equinox with a dance and we begin to flirt in the delicious new light with everything blossoming around us.

We wait for the first full moon after the Equinox which triggers the birds to lay their eggs. The children go looking for the eggs, they love it because they are very good at it, being nimble and quick and able to get into small places and climb the spindliest of branches. They are rewarded with treasures for their skill and self-belief.

Especially good are the wild Goose eggs because they are the biggest and because they are very high in cholesterol. This is the first cholesterol we've had since the last of the meat when Orion set for the last time in early February. It's as though we've had an oil change after the weeks of Spring cleaning, we now have fresh new cholesterol from the very earliest stage of life – the egg. The period of eating only leaves and flowers between the last of the meat and the first of the eggs is the origin of Lent.

The combination of eating the eggs with the Spring leaves is heavenly; the leaves are so fiery and the eggs are so creamy and rich. The bliss of eating this kind of food while filling up with the exciting new hormones of oestrogen and testosterone is the joy we all need and love at this time of year. It's also what the body needs to help it cope with the sudden changes of hormone levels.

Like many animals around us, these hormonal changes trigger us to give birth. Being born while others are bursting with joy must be a lovely way to come into the world and an easier time for the mother to recover after the birth.

There is a whole medicine chest around us for both mother and baby. The lichens which we saved over the Winter from our firewood branches, are used now: Methuselah's Beard lichen is given to the mother after the birth; Black tree lichen mixed with grease and rubbed on to the naval of newborns prevents infections; the juice of Reindeer Lichen is decocted to bathe newborns; Icelandic Moss increases the flow of breast milk, it's also significantly anti-carcinogenic with regards to two breast cancers; Lungwort lichen restores moisture to the tissue that produces breast milk; Fairy Pelt lichen is a remedy for nappy rash. Later, Waxpaper lichen is rubbed on the gums of teething children to make them less restless and sleep.

The woods around us are full of Sphagnum moss which is an anti-septic, soft and highly absorbent, it is the perfect material for use as nappies.

These lichens and mosses only grow high up in the woods. They only grow in places where we'd like to give birth.

As Spring progresses, the babies and mothers become stronger. After six weeks or so, the Spring greens begin to disappear or become too woody to eat. There are no more eggs and the air becomes muggy and hot. Still days bring out a multitude of insects which pollinate the flowers of the fruit trees and they bite us viciously, delighted to be alive. Heaven is about to become hell. We no longer want to be there.

So, we go to where life would be heaven for us again: the sea!

When animals migrate, they don't tend to dawdle, they run. Leaving one season's feeding ground for the next, they barely stop until they reach their destination. For us, leaving the cave on the moor, we would have headed south fairly briskly following the River Dart. It's the quickest way to the sea, it also means we didn't have to carry any food or water.

Beside every river and along the top of every ridge of high land, there is an animal trail, a path that all the animals use. We didn't need canoes, we just followed the path and took the high road because being up high feels good for us. We can see what's coming and there's no danger of getting trapped on a narrow bit of land between a cliff and the river which would make a good hunting spot for another animal.

It takes two days to walk from the cave to the sea and at the half-way point, there is a deep pool in the river where Salmon and Sea Trout rest on their own migratory route. Coming down off the ridge for the first night from the cave, we'd have fished there. Afterwards, no doubt the young people and the children would have jumped from the trees into the river and laughed and splashed about, mad with the deliciousness of cold water after the muggy journey and daring each other on to jump from even higher branches, radiating a happy, competitive energy, everyone loving this place.

Each place has it's challenges, each skill practised has its uses in the next place.

It isn't wise to camp beside a river: there is dampness, there are biting insects in the stagnant places, and there is always the possibility of a flood from rain unseen upriver. And so, further inland and slightly higher up, there is a flat piece of land, a perfect place to feast on the Salmon and Sea Trout and dance and sleep.

In the gloaming of the evening, the melatonin levels increase again, and, mixed with the high testosterone and oestrogen levels of late Spring, the feeling is electric as we take our place in the procession to the river to bow our heads and drink.

Before dawn, the melatonin levels drop off so the feelings of joy surge again making us feel happy to be alive again. The procession to drink begins again and all the other animals and birds are feeling the same kind of buzz.

Another day's walk along the high path and we come running down on to the beach with its glorious blue horizons and fresh sea breeze. It is a heavenly feeling as we know we are going to stay for the whole Summer. Fish only come into the shallows in Summer, seaweed only grows in the Summer, the seashore plants are only juicy enough to eat in the Summer and we only want to be by the sea in the Summer.

We make our shelters out of branches and leaves and as the tide slides back it reveals a treasure chest of food and medicines, beauty treatments and aphrodisiacs.

We are going to conceive on this beach and it is only here that we find the substances needed to prepare our bodies for conception and the food we need to make our bodies the healthiest they can possibly be.

Seaweed contains two important substances needed to prepare the human body for conception: laminarian and fucoidan and they are only found in brown seaweed. Seaweeds are the most powerful foods on Earth.

Because they are so high in iodine, when we eat them our whole body is being healed of infections, cancers that have started, inflammations, parasites or bacteria. Iodine also makes our skin tan easily and safely in the sun.

The sea air contains iodine that has become atomised so that as we breath it, it gets absorbed through the lungs and into the bloodstream, making us feel alive and well.

The gel on seaweeds prevents it from drying out in the sun at every low tide. This gel is completely compatible with our skin making it soft and nourished, healing eczema, psoriasis, cold sores, acne, shingles and dermatitis of all kinds. Our skin and seaweed have an ancient relationship because, millions of years ago when we began to come out of the sea, we must have lain amongst the seaweed for long periods as our lungs and skin adapted to the air and our bodies grew limbs. The gel that protects seaweed protected our skin as it changed and this relationship continues to this day. The gel in the pod at the tip of Bladderwrack contains a powerful healing gel which is always cool, no matter how hot the day and is a fast acting treatment for sunburn.

The sand acts as a powerful exfoliant on our bare feet leaving the skin soft and fully open to absorb the nourishment in the seaweed as we walk across it, like velvet rafts on the sharp rocks.

There is a dreamy quality to hunting for seaweeds, watching their fronds swaying to and fro in deep rock pools at the edge of the sea. Casting one's shadow over the water acts like a daylight torch, making a strip of shade so that we can see into the depths.

We gather small limpets because the larger ones are too chewy to eat and time the gathering of them with their lunar cycles.

We women love processing foods; it soothes our active minds, we love the hard exercise and being in rhythm with each other together, it intensifies the experience to levels which can only be reached if we are working together. Seaweeds raise the metabolism to the highest it can possibly be, giving us energy as though we have the power of the sea itself coursing through our veins: calm and steady and relentless.

Water Lily and Sea Club roots are ready at this time of year, and Reed Mace and a multitude of seed heads jangle like tribal masks in the tall grasses. These are very hard seeds and roots to prepare, and we do it because they are special. This is no ordinary food: Water Lily roots are an aphrodisiac. We pound and sing as the seeds and roots are prepared and ground, our cheeks flush with the physical exertion making us even more beautiful.

As the daylight hours increase, our fertility increases and the excitement that has been growing in us since the first flirtations in Spring would be unbearable now but for the pounding of these seeds and these roots ready for the special feast.

We boil carrageen moss seaweed and rub it into our hair to make it soft and shiny. We place strips of kelp on to our faces to draw out impurities making the skin gleam. We scrub our bodies with Bladderwrack to exfoliate the old skin from our bodies and moisturise it. And as the sun warms the rock-pools, the seaweeds release their vitamins and minerals into the water where our skin is designed to absorb them straight into the bloodstream. Bathing in a sun-warmed rock-pool is pure heaven at the end of a hard day's pounding.

As the full moon rises after the Summer Solstice it becomes the sign for everyone to gather on the beach to party all night. We feed the children a meal of seaweed which makes them sleep, and then we BBQ lobster and crab, mackerel stuffed with Rock Samphire, we eat oysters, bake Water Lily root cakes and wild seed bread to steady our excitement, we dance, we make love.

This party goes on, night after night, for a whole month. The Honeymoon month. The air is warm, the sea is warm, the sand is warm and the night sky is full of shooting stars.

In the first trimester of our pregnancy, we need foods that are rich in Omega 3, Folic Acid and Vitamin A. On the beach we are in the *only* place where there is plenty of all of these: in fish and shellfish and seaweeds. Laminaria seaweeds balance our hormones so that we don't feel sick and the vitamins from the sun strengthen our bodies.

At the Autumn Equinox, the receptor in our eye triggers the Pineal gland to give us a huge increase in melatonin, it makes us want to head inland to hibernate for the Winter. We wait until after the first dark moon after the Equinox, when the first Salmon and Sea Trout return from the sea to swim upriver, to spawn. They come on the highest tides of the year. They are full of caviar which is rich in the substance we need at this time of our pregnancy: Omega 3. Following a trail of caviar is the only way we can be persuaded to leave the beach after such a lovely time.

Before leaving though, we gather the seeds of the wild carrot for the women who did not conceive this time. They will need them during the months ahead because wild carrot seeds are a contraceptive. A teaspoonful is eaten every day for three days after making love and they work by releasing a hormone which thins the lining of the womb so that a fertilised egg will not settle. The wild carrots only grow by the sea and their seeds are ready just when we leave the beach.

Heading back to our Winter cave, up river along the animal trail, we walk more slowly than on the way down because the wild fruits and berries are so tempting. As the sky becomes a much colder blue with the sun so far south, it makes the warm orange of the Rosehips and the deep pinky reds of the Hawberries stand out even more and they flash at us. After gathering several, the dazzling colour combinations of cold blue and warm orangey-reds have pressed their shapes into the rods and cones in the retina of our eyes creating a subliminal message, making it even easier to see them and making it even harder to resist them.

Our blood needs these berries to prepare it for the Winter. The Rosehips and Haws, Sloes and Rowanberries thicken our blood and fortify it with vitamins and minerals, packing them in. Some berries, like Guelder Rose break down the fats of nuts so we can store them on our bodies.

Each year is different but the berries contain just the right amount of the right kinds of substances we need for the kind of Winter we are about to have. If there is going to be a hard Winter of heavy frosts coming, the trees and bushes will produce more berries because they might die. The berries contain their seeds which are spread far and wide by us and by the birds and so ensure the tree will take root somewhere else and survive the Winter.

After eating the berries, we will drop the seed in a perfect "manure parcel" into the ground where we have dug a hole with our foot and we cover it over with earth. It will lie protected and dormant until Spring. As a result of the trees ensuring their own survival by producing more berries, there are more berries for the birds and for us to eat which ensures our survival too and so on.

We are careful where we step as we approach the wild plumb trees because they are always surrounded by badger droppings, full of stones. The wild plumbs have a quick effect on badgers and other small animals, ensuring the seeds are dropped nearby so that the plumb trees can grow together, protecting themselves from the winds they don't like.

Our Winter residence is a cave high up a hill because cold, damp air sinks to the valley floor and freezes. Our cave is surrounded by trees which act like a natural wind break and an umbrella and provides us with firewood, meat, roots and lichens. There is plenty of everything for everyone.

Once installed in the cave, Orion the Hunter rises in the night sky indicating the time to start hunting again. We go out every day, hunting the animals that live in the woods. The meat is often tough because these animals are the older ones, but marinating it in the acidic juices of the wild berries we gather, breaks down the meat's fibres and softens it so we can eat it. The combination of these fruits and these meats ensures the right enzymes are created in our digestive juices for us to fully absorb the nourishment. And wild meat marinated in wild berries is heaven.

On the way back from gathering the food for the day, we carefully select the kind of wood that is right for cooking whatever we have found. For example, if we are to make a meat and root casserole, we want it to simmer on the fire for a long time, so we select some Ash wood branches because they will burn slow and long. If we want to make a cup of tea, we gather pine sticks because these burn hot and fast. If we want to roast some meat, we might use oak, the smoke adding even more flavour, perhaps activating the hormones too.

As armfuls of wood are brought into the cave every day, the lichens are carefully removed and sorted into their kinds and let dry. Lichens are 97% carbohydrate. Little by little, the piles will grow so that when the time comes in Spring there will be enough of each to use.

The colour combinations in the world around us begin to zing.

Yellow and orange leaves increasingly cover the ground, they zing and shimmer at us even in the falling light, lifting our spirits at a time of increased melatonin and the combination is intoxicating. Running across them during the hunt is an extra-ordinary experience, for the hunter and the hunted.

Wild mushrooms seem to "ping" into sight. Being the reproductive organs of the massive mycelium, they are full of hormones. Mycelium is the largest organism on Earth which runs through the ground helping to break down matter. When the mycelium hits an obstacle that it can't cross like a stream or a wood it doesn't like, it sends up a mushroom to send out spores to cross the obstacle. Because fungi are neither plant nor animal but in a kingdom of their own, consuming them lifts us into another realm too.

Some Oak leaves emit a sweet smelling hormone as they turn brown. It smells like candyfloss and all the animals like it too. This scent is so appealing that we want to catch it again, and so we sniff the air harder to catch some more. It has a soporific effect on humans and on animals. In early Autumn when there are only a few dried Oak leaves, it acts as a trigger for us to get in our supplies for the Winter but as Autumn progresses and there are more brown oak leaves, the effect becomes stronger and increases our sense of urgency to get home and hibernate. Small animals are seen dragging these special Oak leaves into their burrows, ensuring a deep sleep throughout the Winter.

The Oak leaf scent slows everyone down at the same rate so nobody has an advantage over anyone else. Nature, the fairest of them all.

The lowering angles of sunlight flash into our eyes through the bushes and trees, like a magician's trick, they make things disappear and reappear as we are momentarily blinded. Within a few weeks, all of the leaves and undergrowth will disappear completely.

The deeper we go into Winter, the less sunlight there is and the more melatonin is produced by the Pineal gland, the link between our bodies and the skies. With so much melatonin in us, those who didn't conceive will stop menstruating altogether.

For those who are heavily pregnant, there are thick bear skin rugs by the fire to curl up in, roasted red meat and sweet roots to eat and plenty of time to doze in a warm, dry cave in the quiet depths of Winter. The combination of eating so much protein and carbohydrate together at the same meal slows down our metabolism, piles on the fat and makes us feel sleepy. Heaven. And the black and white drama of everyday life is projected large and comical on to the cave walls around us to inform and amuse us.

Plants survive the Winter by storing all their energy in their roots or bulbs, tubers or rhizomes. Children love digging for them because they never know what they're going to find or how big they're going to be or what they're going to look like. Roots are golden presents hidden in the heavily scented wrappings of the earth. River-rolled stones are warmed by the fire to be held tightly by anyone coming in with cold hands.

This thinning of the roots helps the plants too by making room for new ones to grow in the Spring. The plants are resting but they are strong and determined to live and they pass on this kind of energy to us when we eat their roots. Along with protein and carbohydrates, we need vitamin C, too. The Winter leaves of the Lady's Smock are full of vitamin C. The undigested stomach contents of the Caribou are full of vitamin C. It tastes like cake. Perhaps the other animals provide the same nourishment.

With all the undergrowth gone, the hunters can see the animals more clearly now. The herds survive the Winter by shedding the slow ones. The cold makes the slow ones even slower and so making it possible for a hunter to catch them. No matter how fast he is, a hunter can only catch the slowest of his prey, even if he's the fastest cat on Earth.

When an animal is hunted, adrenaline is pumping through its body. Adrenaline is a euphoriant and a painkiller. At the point of capture, the animal experiences the most amount of adrenaline it can ever have and so the euphoria and lack of pain make it rise into Heaven.

Children love being chased. They shriek with delight and want to do it again and again. It fills them with adrenaline as they practise their dodging and weaving. They are very ticklish on the back of their neck and their sides and on the soles of their feet because these are the places that a carnivore would be most likely to catch them. The exquisite feeling of being caught during a game of chase with the ecstasy of something breathing down their neck is almost unbearably good, for good reason.

Nature encourages a carnivore to bite the neck by providing a burst of sweet hormonal juices in reward as the spinal column is severed. It helps to replenish the spent energy. In turn, this action paralyses the prey and ensures there is no pain.

Children love carnivores. They take replicas of them to bed to cuddle. They can't sleep without them. They are all warm and cuddly and make them feel loved and taken care of and that's what they need to see coming towards them if they have fallen down a cliff and broken their leg. They don't want to see a rook swooping down to peck out their eyes. Children don't take rooks to bed.

The animals need the hunters to keep them strong and we need the animals to keep *us* strong. We help each other. We can only take as much as we can carry and so we cannot take more than we need. As much as we can carry is as much as a family can eat.

Every part of the animal is used. The long leg sinews are pounded to separate the fibres and make cordage. The hides are prepared to make leather for clothes. If we have too many skins to cope with, we can take them down to the bottom of the hill and put them in the freezer.

Clothing made of skins goes hard if it gets wet and it's very uncomfortable to wear. So tanning the hide will ensure the leather stays soft even in the rain. By soaking the skin in the brains of the animal, the acid in the brains breaks down the fibres to make the leather stay soft.

Every animal has just enough brains to tan its own hide.

After all the fat and meat has been scraped off on one side and the hair and epidermis scraped off the other, the hide is soaked in the animal's brains mashed up in water. Then it's strung up on a frame and with one person on one side and another person on the other, the fibres are worked into by pressing them and pushing them with the shoulder blade of the animal, to release the water. We sing in rhythm, the beat of our paddles hitting the hide to keep us in time, our spirits are lifted as our whole bodies work steadily for hours and hours, turning drudgery into fun, hide into leather, straw into gold.

The lifted voices of our singing, echo through the cave making musical harmonies all around us and back at us and the beating of our paddles acts as a drumbeat.

Every activity has its own song because every job needs a different kind of rhythm to turn the raw material into the useful. A job that requires a slow gentle rhythm to begin with and then builds steadily to a massive climax at the end is accompanied by a song which tells the story of two people who meet and fall in love; a job that requires a slow steady rhythm for hours and hours has a song that tells the story of a family's history stretching back many generations in time. As the children play around their mothers, they are learning all the lessons that anyone ever needed to know.

To make a piece of leather soft enough to wear, we need the energy of both men and women. We have very different kinds of energy but they are both needed equally. When men go hunting they often have to move slowly but fully alert for long hours then have to act very swiftly, exert a huge amount for force, then use steady strength to get the meat home by which time they are completely spent. Their kind of energy provides the skin.

Women's energy is more even; we can work rhythmically and steadily for hours and hours and hours. Together we provide the two kinds of energy that are needed to make a piece of leather soft enough to last for a hundred years.

Hunting and gathering gives us such beautiful thoughts and the dreams we have after eating wild food are beautiful too. As the Winter Solstice approaches we prepare ourselves to receive the gifts of this special time. As the full moon rises, it induces a hormone which swells the base of the deer's antlers. The mighty stags lower their heavy heads for the last time and lay down their antlers. Lifting their heads free from them, they leap on their way as though they are flying.

The hunters go out into the moonlight and gather these antlers and return with them to the cave. The red and white spotted mushrooms (the Fly Agaric) that have been dried and saved for the longest nights when all is still, are eaten now. They give us dreams of flying through the air with the deer to distant lands where we are given gifts of new knowledge and understanding. These we bring home to share with each other in ever deepening acts of kindness and love.

When the relationship between a living being and Nature changes from being an equal amount of give and take, to being when it need more from Nature than it can give in return, it dies. On our daily round, we and all the animals know where the bogs are, where the cliff edges are, where the carnivores live, where all the dangers are and so we avoid them because we want to live. But when we want to die, we know where to go.

Heavy frosts occur on the starriest of nights, taking countless lives with them. Older animals and plants and humans too, hear the lullaby of the stars and feel the pull of their call to sleep, they beckon to them sweetly. The scene of a billion celestial diamonds is matched only by the number of souls rising into heaven that night. A starry sky is Nature's graveyard. No wonder it's always so peaceful. And so magical.

Orion the Hunter will soon be disappearing from our skies again but until it does our hunters will step out into this magical land to send the last of the old animals on their way. We gather Snowdrops and Daffodil bulbs, Celandines and Arum Lily for when our hunters return because these, the first flowers and leaves of Spring, are all medicines to heal their wounds.

We fit perfectly into this land and this land fits perfectly into us.

As hunter-gatherers we live peacefully, playing our part and being rewarded as we do so with revelations and heavenly experiences every day of the year, every day of our lives without destroying anything at all.

*

As we follow The Ring of the Wild Food Year, the wild food cleans our blood in the Spring, heals our blood in the Summer, fortifies our blood in the Autumn, and rests our blood in the Winter.

Keeping our blood healthy is the reason why we are on Earth. We are the keepers of our family blood. What we put into our blood or what we take out, gets passed on to our children. Then they become the keepers, adding their stuff to it before passing it on to their children.

Our job is to keep it clear of debris so that it can be the best carrier of goodness that it can be. We are simply vessels so that blood, the richest of our hormonal juices, remains on Earth. Nature needs the hormones that our blood releases into the air, so that they will mix with hormones from the other animals, and from the plants, the trees, the flowers and insects, and gullies and creeks and soil, to become the breath of life. To become love.

The Ring of the Wild Food Year

Epilogue

It's been 15 years now, almost to the day, since I returned from Australia to learn the wild food of my own country and to find out what had really happened to separate us from Nature.

I'm glad I chose to explore down this road, it has been a far richer journey than I ever imagined.

I hunt and gather wild food as much as I can now and I have been lucky that others have wanted to learn it too. When they come with me on a wild food walk they too find themselves stepping into a much more magical world than they ever knew was there.

When you realise how much we loved hunting and gathering and how easily we have been conned out of everything we held most dear, you can begin to understand the depth of sadness that lives within us in this country. This wound is constantly kept open and fed on by advertisers sowing seeds of doubt and so breaking our spirits still further. I wish it would stop.

But, all is not lost. Nature is the greatest superpower on Earth and we belong within it. No matter what happens with climate change, there will always be wild food. Even if you just add one thing from the wild to your daily food, be it a few nettles or dandelion leaves into your soup, you will give yourself and the world what it really needs: by eating wild food, you are putting back the apple and regaining your passion. The passion of Nature.

Ffyona Campbell, Devon. November 2012

Appendix 1

Notes, Observations, Experiences

This is a collection of some of my discoveries and thoughts which didn't make it into the format of the rest of the book but I still love them and wanted to share them, so I have added them here at the end, in no particular order.

*

The strangeness and sense of incompleteness that happens so often in dreams these days I suspect is because that's the weirdness of what the plant or animal has lived through in its life and that's the kind of energy it's got that it has passed on to you.

After eating wild food for about two months, I noticed there was a very distinctive pattern to my dreams, they had become vivid and delicious to be in. They would always begin with a challenge that I faced but one which I couldn't possibly overcome. I'd be saying to myself that if only I had a sword, for example, I'd be able to cope. And I'd look down and see that I had a sword and that I'd always had one but didn't realise it was there. I'd take it out and find that I actually had the ability to use it even though I'd never seen it before. And I found I had courage too, courage that I didn't know I had and with this new found strength and skill I overcame the challenge and after feeling completely satisfied, amazed and deeply proud of myself, I would wake up.

If you look at the challenge a wild shoot or a wild animal has to overcome and then it finds it's equipped with thorns, or horns, finding it already knows how to use them and that they work, you'll see there is a distinct and logical connection between this and the dreams I have when I eat them.

Now think of the dreams you have after eating modern food and how you wake up just before something nice is going to happen. Look at the life of the plant or animal you've eaten: they are forced to grow in a controlled environment and never allowed to shoot into flower or make love. How much can be understood in a dream where you're always being nipped in the bud?

As a general rule, if you can gather a lot of something very easily, you can eat a lot of it. If it takes you a long time to gather something, for example, to get the nut out of a thistle, you can't eat a lot of it because it's too rich for us.

There is an excitement that comes over some people these days when they discover they are surrounded by the most delicious plants they've ever eaten. And it's all free. Even though I show them how to carefully pick each one, how care must be taken not just for the plant but also to avoid picking one of the poisonous leaves which grow amongst them, their excitement becomes too great and they are driven to break Natures law.

To be more specific I have noticed this only in some men, never yet in a woman. After overhearing one man say to his friend "let's come back later and get all of this", and another on the beach stuffing vast quantities of seaweed into a bag which he would never need; and then on a wild mushroom walk meeting one of my students with a basket full of fungi saying I shouldn't bother to go back the way he'd been because he'd picked them all after he'd agreed to only ever take a third, I despaired. I felt I wasn't equipped to stop them from taking more than they need and I was tempted to ban men from my walks.

But then I remembered to tell the story about the Pygmies going up the tree for honey and how there is always a woman at the bottom of the tree reminding them to leave some for the bees. And they laugh in understanding, because now they are not ashamed of their enthusiasm.

The moment you stop yourself from taking all the wild food is the moment when you actually believe that Nature will provide for you. Because you have left some wild food, there *will* always be plenty. Believing that Nature will always provide for you is a very practical kind of faith.

I noticed that the best Spring leaves and flowers grow at the top of the hill near my house. Every Spring I marvelled at the lushness of these plants and I loved gathering them there on the top of the hill because the views were so wonderful and the sky so big and open after being inside all Winter.

When it came time for me to try and figure out where the cave was that we lived in as hunter-gatherers for the Winter and Spring, I knew it would be up a hill because cold air sinks and I knew it would be on or near Dartmoor because it was wooded then. So, I rang the archaeology department of the Dartmoor National Park to ask them if they knew of any caves where stone tools had been found? They said yes, they did know of one. It was right beside the place where I had been gathering Spring leaves.

I found the remains of the cave. It's very sad that it has all been quarried out for use as building materials. The road going up to the remains of the cave is called Fairy's Hall. I think that might have been the name of the cave itself. What a beautiful place it must have been to be called Fairy's Hall.

In the months after I left Africa and was living in the Welsh hills, I missed my life out there so much I decided to try and bring it to life again by doing the things I'd seen African women doing. One of those, was to balance a bucket of water on my head. Some amazing things started to happen.

Take a drying up cloth, roll it into a sausage then curl it round into what the African women call a "halo." Put the halo on the top of your head. Then fill a round bucket half-full of water (and if you think we didn't have buckets when we were hunter-gatherers, think again). Then place the bucket on top of the halo. You will notice straight away that your chin goes up so that the top of your head is level. If you have been a bit miserable or depressed, it might have been some time since you held your head up. This action alone will start making you feel better.

Then comes the business of taking your hands away. But as soon as you do the bucket starts to wobble. It does this for two reasons: either the water isn't horizontal or you don't believe you can do it.

In order for water to be completely horizontal it must be on something which is completely vertical. Being vertical is a process of the the water itself sending a rod down through your spine making it straight. It's not a material rod of course, it's the rod that makes the horizons of the sea keep straight.

If you relax while it is going down through your back and let the water's energy find its way, you will find it's like having an amazingly gentle but highly effective chiropractic treatment because it makes some muscles relax, others it tightens up. It does it very quickly, like water finding its way down a hill.

So, at this point your head is held high and your neck and shoulders are relaxed. I have taught this to people and watched their transformation and within moments they are looking so beautiful. Elegant and graceful and poised.

Now, you must believe in yourself. If you don't, you will have to walk around for the rest of your life with your hands on the bucket. Like riding a bicycle you have to believe that an invisible force is going to help you. It's interesting that believing in yourself is actually believing in the invisible forces of Nature.

You banish all negative thoughts and give yourself only positive affirmations and soon you will be standing poised and graceful with your arms down by your side.

Now you must take a step forward. Because you are barefoot, you will want to see what you are going to put your foot on but with a bucket of water on your head, you can only see from about three feet in front of you. You can't see what you're about to step on. So, you have to take a leap of faith. When you do, you will notice that the first sensation your feet tell you about is good. It only tells you the good news of how warm and soft the ground is, it doesn't tell you how cold or sharp it is. The pleasing warmth under your feet makes you smile inside and you are looking even more beautiful.

Because you can't anticipate anything bad, your feet relax and do what feet do best – seek out the *lovely* sensations on the ground and tell you about them. If something is sharp, your feet gently curl around them and because they are relaxed they are pliable: when they are stiffened by fear they are not pliable. All the animals are barefoot and they can run over anything, because they don't look down. Successful barefoot walking is all about anticipation.

And as you walk, the water keeps your shoulders stilled and sways your hips from side to side. It is the most beautiful feeling because you are in perfect balance, you are believing in yourself and you are anticipating only good.

All that from just a bucket of water and a drying up cloth.

Feet are amazingly misunderstood. When they are cold they go red. I discovered why this is after nine months of being barefoot in the Welsh hills. By the time Winter came, my feet had become huge and I often wondered whether this was normal or not. But then I saw a photograph of the last of our native hunter-gatherers who had lived on the Island of St.Kilda off the west coast of Scotland. There was a bunch of them, women of all ages, all of them were barefoot and all of them had feet as swollen as mine. None of them looked concerned. So, I knew that I was on the right track.

Feet are made of tissue which is designed to swell with blood when they get cold. So, if you put shoes and socks on, your feet can't swell up and so they stay cold. This is what people mean when they say they have poor circulation. Take off your shoes and socks and let the blood flow in and they will be warm again.

Aphrodite the Goddess of Love was said to be born of the froth of the sea and having a seaweed spa bath in a sun warmed rock pool, makes a woman feel and look like the Goddess herself.

In the book The Horse Whisperer by Monty Roberts, he recalls watching the wild Mustang in the desert. He noticed what happened when a wild horse was mortally wounded in a fight with another stallion – the wounded animal turned towards an area where Roberts had seen some mountain lions. He witnessed the horse put himself into the right place to be killed quickly. Animals can commit suicide.

I once lived in a cottage in the middle of a field of sheep with only a small footpath leading across the hill to my door. I had got used to the sounds of the sheep in the night. A few weeks after the lambs were born it started to rain and it didn't stop raining for 9 days and nights. Then the temperature plummeted while they were still wet and it started to freeze. I wondered what sound the sheep would be making in these conditions. Would they be whimpering? No.

Whimpering is the dinner bell for monsters.

I listened carefully and realised that a single, very deep "baaar" was coming from every ewe in turn around the field. It was a strong, slow sound they made. It was reassuring and warm and it reached every corner of the field and it was saying to the lambs that we are all here and that all is well. It made them relax so they didn't tense up and start shivering. They were singing them a lullaby.

I was making rag dolls out of completely natural materials, stuffed with wool I'd found on gorse bushes up on the moor. I wanted to dye them and so make them lovely but I was worried they might be poisonous to children. I happened to meet a commercial dyer and asked him if natural dyes are poisonous. He replied that all natural dyes are toxic and shouldn't be used for making rag dolls for children.

Toxic? That's a *very* strong word. It stood out like a flag because I could see how easy it would be to sow that seed of doubt in the minds of natural dyers and so get them to switch to the new commercial dyes. It was such a strong word that I had a feeling it was masking something important. Like, could these plants have actually been *medicines* instead?

I contacted Jenny Dean, Britain's leading expert on natural dyes and asked her if the dye plants could have been used as medicines. She sent me back a lovely letter saying that I was absolutely right. In fact, that's how we discovered they gave a dye in the first place because we were using those plants as medicines and noticed they gave a good colour. She suggested I take this one step further and cross reference a list of dye plants with a book on herbal medicine to see what the plants were used for.

I cross referenced all of them and found that they are all medicines for the skin. When we had a skin problem, we soaked our under-clothes in a tea of that wild plant and "wore" the medicine. The dye seeped into our skin and healed the problem. We saw it also gave a lovely colour and so later went back to that plant for it's colour.

So, the warning away from something natural, was the sign that pointed to useful forgotten knowledge.

I was at the gym and I noticed that most people were wearing blue but they were all different kinds of blue. The red-head suited one kind of blue, the blonde suited another and so on. I wondered about this.

The answer became clear when I had my colours "done" by a colour practitioner who held different coloured scarves up to my face to see which ones suited me.

By the end of the session I was amazed to see that all the colours I suited were of the west coast of Scotland – the soft, dusky colours of the mists, the heathers, the peaty earth, the hazy sea. My father's family is from the west coast of Scotland and I have his colouring. That I suit the colours of my homeland makes sense if you look at it from a hunter-gatherer point of view – I would be completely camouflaged in my landscape. Important if you are trying to hunt something or trying not to be caught.

Then I realised that what makes those colours in the landscape is the composition of minerals in the soil, the very minerals that I am made up of because I eat those plants that grow in it and I eat those animals who eat those plants that grown in it. And so I belong to that landscape, I am made up of that landscape, I am part of it and I become invisible in it.

When we were hunter-gatherers we lived in a clan where everyone had the same colouring and the same kind of physique. When people are at their most beautiful it's because they are happy and I think that when we are with people who all look like us, we don't feel negative about ourselves, it takes out the sting of not having a physique like someone else or not having their colouring. We also feel happy because we are exactly what's needed in that environment. Being needed is such a fundamental part of being happy.

The more wild food I eat, the more camouflaged I become. In Spring my hair takes on a slightly pink hue and I noticed this same hue on a woman on one of my wild food walks. I asked her if she was already eating wild food and she was, a lot of it. In the Autumn, I noticed that my hair was turning more chestnut brown the more wild mushrooms I ate, I was quickly becoming camouflaged in the woods, like them.

I've noticed that if I wear the colours of the woods when I am walking through them, I disappear, as though I'm wearing a cloak of invisibility, even to myself because I don't even see my arms swinging. But if I walk through the woods wearing red, I feel like a piece of litter. I keep seeing my arms and legs and it distracts my eye so that I can't relax and so I can't see into the natural world.

It must be the same for animals – wild animals have colouring that camouflages them and so they must disappear even to themselves as they run. But modern dogs have ridiculous colouring and so it probably distracts them. You can see some dogs these days have completely lost the plot, mentally.

Wool has an ancient partnership with the wind and rain. Instead of blocking it out, wool allows the wind in and in turn the wind swells up the fibres making them even warmer at every gust. Lanolin is the substance in the wool which keeps it clean and conditioned. It isn't like oil because it dissolves instantly in water so that when it rains the lanolin is being run down the length of the wool, washing it and conditioning it. So, when it rains the sheep are having a shower, with soap. You can take a piece of fleece, dip it in water and wash your windows with it, or use it to remove tannin from tea cups, nothing sparkles like using a bit of fleece with its lanolin on.

I was thinking about why Africans are black and I realised that it's not just so they don't get burned, it's because it's so hot in Africa, and they spend a lot of their time sitting in the shade. They are hunters, by being black and sitting in the black shade, the animals can't see them.

Colour combinations play such an important role when gathering wild food. I've noticed that when I see gold on green I am automatically on the look out for wild mushrooms; reddish purple on grey says look out for dulse seaweed; orange on cold blue says rosehips. Their colours call to us for a reason, they are calling to us to eat them because the plants need our input to help them spread. Perhaps the colour's song is the call of the wild.

I have often thought there is music coming from the sun.

Blackberries make your arms grow longer. Have you ever noticed how the biggest ones always grow just out of reach? I often think it's because they are for the giants, though they fell during our wars, their food is still there, waiting for them to return.

When talking to Aborigines they refer to their ancient teachers and I realised that yet again we miss the important bit of information because we are relating it to modern religions – Christianity, Islam, Judaism, all refer to a teachers that lived thousands of years ago. Aborigines are talking about ancient teachers but they are still alive all around us – the wild animals and the plants. They taught us our lessons thousands of years ago but they are still here beside us.

Watching the seagulls flying for fun, I realised they are doing it to unwind after the hunt. Each swoop and curve made seemingly for pure joy, is actually releasing the tension in their bodies. By watching them with awe and wonder, they enter me and so they teach me. They are saying that I must do my special thing to release tension after the day's work. I wondered what it is that people can do which would give us this much relaxation?

And I realised that the thing we must do is to dance. No wonder the hunter-gatherers always dance by the fire after the hunt, they are relieving the muscles they used and they do it by telling the story of the day's hunt, using the movements they made while hunting but softening them now, using the rhythm of their excited hearts during the hunt as the drumbeat to relax them now. They do this at the end of every day and so they wake without tension, ready and refreshed to begin again.

I'm sure that dancing also relaxes us so that our hormones can flow more easily, that love can come in and flow out. And that's why the seagulls fly for pleasure, they are balancing their hormones, unwinding so that they can let the love flow in and out of every cell and every feather so they can allow the hormones of the world to flow through them the next day and so they can find the fish that are emitting their hormones of distress. It does seem right when you look at them and can feel them in you, it feels so purifying, what they are doing.

I remember a Peruvian Indian telling me that in Peru dancing is medicine and it has the same name.

I'm sure that slugs are actually the wolves of the plant world because they go straight for the plants that have been put where Man wanted them to be and so they are emitting their distress. Gathering wild food I have very rarely seen any slugs at all (except on the very best mushrooms) but they have been all over my garden any time I have tried to impose my will on where the plants grow.

I can feel the love pouring out of a spider when, after being found trapped in the bath all night, I have offered it a firm foothold on a napkin and then taken it slowly outside and laid it on the grass and watched as it takes a step off the napkin and the relief floods through it and it finds a dark spot under a leaf and rests. It's the same with insects crashing against the window trying to find the way out. If you open your heart to how they are feeling, you will hear them asking you if you know the way out. Bees only buzz when you're there.

Watch what happens when you open the window and they fly out, there is always a dip in their flight as they still think they are going to be restricted by something invisible but then they aren't and their expression as they fly up, up and away, is pure open joy at being free and rightness is restored to the world. The ancient ones are all around us, living the life that we once lived and long for now.

When I look up at the stars at night, I don't feel small and insignificant as some people do. I say to myself "If I can see that star then that star can see me! I must be pretty amazing!"

If there is only one of something in Nature it's big enough for everyone to share.

For about six weeks recently, I stopped eating wheat, dairy and sugar. I wanted to feel the full hormonal excitement of the seaweed and realised that these modern foods interfere with the hormonal balance.

As the days went by I felt myself becoming much clearer in thought and movement and the blissful feelings returned at every wild food meal. But one week-end life got in the way and I ate wheat, dairy and sugar at every meal for two days. Not only did I get the expected stomach cramps, but I got sunburnt. I've been brown as a berry all Summer. I strongly suspect that the acidity in my body caused by those hormone hijackers, caused my skin to burn.

Talking this over with my daughter, she mentioned that on a recent three day camp they were given a lot of dairy to eat (far more than she'd ever had) and she was badly burned on her shoulders - which had never happened to her.

We know that what makes us brown is a hormone. It would make sense then that if we are eating a hormonal food - which milk is more than anything else - then the hormones we need to produce could be affected. After all, babies don't tend to tan and when you consume dairy products you are eating food meant for a baby.

I think it's quite likely that we get sunburned in our own climate because we eat dairy products.

When out for a walk in mid-Autumn, I took off my sunglasses and let the sunlight flash into the corner of my eye as I walked along past the hedgerows. As I relaxed and let the light in, I noticed that the partial blinding in one eye at every flash actually feels amazing. It made me realise that something important was happening.

This is what it feels like when the sun is triggering the special receptors in our eyes to trigger the Pineal gland. But it is often at this point that we put on sunglasses. And when we go inside at dusk, we put on electric light.

Many people suffer from Season Affective Disorder during all the changes of seasons and the symptoms are: sleeping too much, having little energy, feeling depressed and feeling anxious. The modern treatments are: light therapy, anti-depressant drugs, cognitive analytical therapy, ionized-air administration, and carefully timed supplementation of the hormone melatonin.

I wonder, if you take your sunglasses off and go out for a walk every evening to let the sunlight in to regulate your body's natural response to the changing seasons, whether you will feel better. And if, when you go inside, you light a candle instead of switching on the electric light.

"Why are there more spiders now?" I asked a group of school children in late September. They didn't know and neither did their teacher but they had all noticed them so, I showed them how to find the answer by using hunter-gatherer thinking - *the thinking that makes sense of Nature*.

Let's start from what we are *actually* experiencing:

I have noticed spiders in my house weaving webs across corners in the ceiling and I have noticed spiders webs in the garden and in the woods mostly where I crash into them with my face or where I am about to put my hand to get a large juicy blackberry. They look like nets and they are very strong and sticky. I have also noticed slow moving flies in my house banging about on furniture. They seem drowsy. Is there a connection between the two?

Yes, spiders eat flies.

Why would they be out catching them now more than during the Spring and Summer? Because the flies are coming to the end of their lives now before the Winter and they crash into things, they are trying to die. So, the spiders, triggered by their banging, put out their nets in places that flies might crash into, so they can catch them. Does this make sense? Yes.

Spiders are the fishermen of the sky.

Wild animals live like the richest people in the world. They own their own homes. They live in the very best places often with a different residence for every season. The things in their homes are made of 100% natural materials. They do a job they love. They eat the finest food. They are accepted and respected and needed. They are confident and have very high self-esteem. They are the healthiest they can possibly be. They are beautiful. They are free to make love to whomever they like. They are free of any master. They don't pay taxes.

Farmed animals don't own their own homes. They rarely live in the best places. They are surrounded by things made of plastic. They are not doing the job they want to do. They are forced to eat what their keeper offers. They are needed but only if they conform to others' ideas of what they should be and what they should look like. They are often fearful.

They are often unhealthy - cow pats are diarrhoea (*frequent and copious discharge of abnormally liquid faeces*). They are too heavy to move easily or too hot in their wool. Their keeper removes their male protectors, forcing them to make love to whomever he chooses. They pay the highest tax - their babies are taken away to be eaten.

Wild animals are hunter-gatherers.

It is in the hormonal experience that all is revealed and understood.

The incense in church smells like the breath of the trees at night when they release their scent. It's so different from the scent of the day because they have changed their breathing. The magic of the evening and the dawn is brought on because this is the point of change. Changing from breathing in oxygen to breathing out oxygen, must be caused by hormones, triggered by sunlight.

The whole world works on hormones, they are the juice of the world. Healthy people look juicy. The juice of the world makes love and magic. Modern food and machines suppress or interfere with the hormones of everything. Electric light, sugar, wheat, dairy, no exercise, sitting down a lot, never being outside smelling the hormones on the air, year in year out, leads to despair. But what makes the hormones become more balanced is physical exercise to speed up the metabolism, light from the sun and moon; if you are inside all the time, the sun and moon can't regulate your body and so your body can't function properly.

The variations in life forms have come because of a life saying to itself "I *can't* do this. But, I *can* do *this*!" Aaha! Is the sound of evolution.

Hunting and gathering is the pot of gold at the end of the rainbow.

People say that "Man has always sought knowledge and that's why we developed and progressed to the people we are today." And yet most people know very little about how things work, it's not important knowledge we've gained by going down this road.

If your hair is greasy from sugar and your eye lids swollen from dairy, your skin flushed red from wine and speckled and broken veined from wheat. You consume all these things for comfort. Why do you need all this comfort? Because you think you're so far away from what would comfort you every minute of the day and in abundance and without any strings – Nature and Natures' food. "Comfort me with wild food" and your hair will glisten and your eye lids sink back in and your skin glow and your whole being will pulse with the peace and power of Nature.

The experience of believing and disbelieving is on either side of every invisible force of Nature; some of these forces haven't yet been detected by science, but we can still feel them ourselves.

In the modern world you have to study what other people have done and thought, before you can add your own thoughts. But in Nature you learn directly from your own experience from the start.

After having a bath of seaweed, I feel the world is more colourful, I feel less fug in my head and my feet are tingling.

If you eat the wild food of your environment you will be the healthiest you can possibly be and you will feel it's strength and elements in your veins.

Dancing is jumping up and down like being shaken in a bottle, all the juices released and going into the blood and the muscles. It's the same action as the tribal dances. You see birds bobbing up and down on a branch. I wonder if they are doing the same thing.

The most comforting food comes at the scariest of times. The shimmery, shaking, frightening face masks I saw in the grasses last Summer were the seed heads which, having been droopy, suddenly seemed to dry out and so stand up and fan out and shake themselves of their seeds. I have a feeling we made masks like them at this time of year and rattled them around us in dances. Makes me realise that each of the tribal dances we see express the essence of what's going on in the bigger cycles so that we become part of it.

All the processes of the world are learned year by year as you grow up and so you can't know it all until you are old.

The more you hunt and gather wild food, the more you will perfect it to a fine art. The Aborigines know that when they are far inland and they see a particular white butterfly, they should head for the sea because the fish will be at their best and coming in to the shallows. I have heard that the Tulip tribe of Washington used the appearance of the white pine butterfly to let them know they should head to the sea for the return of the Chinook Salmon. Maybe it's the same.

The more wild food you eat the more of the realms you can see. No wonder the farmers can't see them – they're eating what they farm so they can't see them and because they can't see them, they farm.

The sweet smell that dogs have when they are happy and that humans have when they are happy and that pigs have when they are happy, comes from the hormones in the blood. And since good smells come from good thoughts and bitter smells come from bitter thoughts, when someone smells sweet, that's because they are thinking sweetly. This is the origin of perfume.

When dogs smell the urine of other dogs on street corners what they really smell is the hormones in the urine and therefore the emotional state of that dog. Pigs have a reputation for stinking, because they are unhappy being cooped up like that.

The wild hormones get you into being accepted by Nature.

You want to believe in something? There's nothing you can trust more than Nature.

The last vestige of the wild is clustered around the churches. The churches were always built where we were feasting and making merry as hunter-gatherers. So, if you want to find the wild food in your area, go to the oldest church and look for the features in the surrounding landscape that would have drawn the animals or birds or fish to gather there. When the supermarket food runs out, the church will be your guide as to where the wild food can be found, leading us to salvation in the end!

Nobody can stop you eating wild food. It will make you feel good. And nobody can stop you! Not even the EU!

The rich rely on demotivated people to buy their wares. The more de-motivated they can make them, the more they will buy.

When foxes are domesticated they produce lower levels of hormones than wild ones. When you smell a fox, it smells very strong, that's because the fox is *feeling* very strong.

French cooking is hormonal – they ride a wave of their juices.

In the western world, it's a designer's job to stimulate a desire that can never be satisfied.

Nowadays, people can't say "we can never go back".

Taming animals turns them into beggars.

Modern food is so more-ish because it creates an instant hormonal imbalance and craving. Hormonal food out of place makes us feel negative – Nature's way of saying "don't do that".

In an open topped aquarium I noticed the sharks and the rays went round and round the outside in an anti-clockwise direction pushing themselves out of the water looking for the way out even if it meant going up into the air to try and find it. The octopus was asleep, trying to find the way out that way.

Farming breeds out the physical ability to get out of the field.

Of all the billions of grains of sand on the beach, not one of them is the same. Now that's an achievement. The idea of making things identical is so boring, yet this is what modern Man prides himself on that he brought to the world.

When we penned in animals, we penned in ourselves with their needs. We made them passive and dependant and more easily malleable and we did this to ourselves too.

After eating wild food, one's bodily functions smell very sweet. Because of the hormones.

I'd rather eat the plant that is as determined, resilient and as fast as a dandelion pushing up through tarmac, than something without gumption.

Our children are growing up in a world where they don't know what gumption is.

How to separate from the modern world at any moment of the day or night: just look at something natural and let your mind quieten and open. It helps to be out of a town because there are only human hormones in town, maybe that's why people feel the need to vie with each other over material things, because there are no other hormones in the air to balance them with.

The key to total freedom forever is what we're all looking for in the modern world, hunter-gatherers have it right now.

The secrets of Nature are like a flower that never stops opening.

Wild animals don't worry that they'll never find another meal because they are designed to a do a job they were evolved to do and they wouldn't have evolved to do it if it didn't need to be done. It's in the doing of the job that gives it the food. His security and assurance of a job for life is because he exists.

Animals communicate with their thoughts and their smells which are their hormones which are their emotions. They don't need words. So are they more or less skilled than Man? You don't see any misunderstandings between animals, they don't have a Police force or a court system. Maybe we learned to use words so that we could lie to each other. Wild animals don't lie to each other. Maybe the first words came with the penning in of animals for the first time, suddenly the relationship is based on a lie: the shepherd says, "Don't worry, I won't hurt you, I will look after you and protect you." But he's going to take away their babies and eat them.

600 people killed themselves in Scotland last year. I bet they would have loved hunting and gathering.

We know from our own experience that time isn't uniform – some minutes are much longer than others. Science isn't human experience. But it is only through human experience that we can *understand* anything.

The Avon lady is going up the Amazon telling the women they work so hard they should treat themselves to a lipstick. Suddenly their work seems hard, they feel hard done by, the only thing that can help them is the lipstick and soon the saleswoman will have moved on and she leaves behind her a trail of discontented women. And once the women are discontent, everyone in the family will be too. Welcome to the modern world.

We've had 4,000 years of people telling us what we are experiencing even if it's something that we're not. For example, people will swear by wearing synthetic waterproofs even though when they take them off they are sodden wet inside and they wouldn't want to put that garment on again to go back outside. But wool keeps us warm and dry even when it's 40% wet and you'd still want to put it back on again, but people will tell you that wool doesn't work. Even when you're standing in front of them in the pouring rain wearing wool and not getting wet.

It's important to strengthen the Pineal gland. People who have the highest rates of breast cancer are airhostesses because their melatonin levels are all over the place with shift work and time changes. Take off your sunglasses and throw out your alarm clock, light a candle instead of an electric light, look after the link between you and the skies and it will look after you.

SURVIVAL INTERNATIONAL

Survival International is the only charity campaigning for the rights of tribal peoples worldwide.

Survival was founded in 1969 in response to the secret genocide of Amazonian Indians. Over the last 40 years Survival has campaigned relentlessly for tribal lives and lands, and to permanently eradicate racist misconceptions.

From the Guarani in Brazil, to the Bushmen in Botswana, tribal peoples all over the world are under threat from material and cultural 'progress'.

Please help us to ensure a future for these highly diverse and intricate peoples. If you haven't done so already, please visit the Survival website www.survivalinternational.org and find out more about their current campaigns. Please also consider giving to Survival. Survival refuses government funding which means it relies on its supporters for everything it does. Your contribution, however small, will allow them to help tribal peoples gain the respect and equality that is rightfully theirs in the 21st century.

FOR MORE COPIES OF THE HUNTER-GATHERER WAY

If you would like to order further copies of this book, please email: wildfoodwalks55@gmail.com.
If you have enjoyed it, why not leave a comment on the Facebook page: The Hunter-Gatherer Way by Ffyona Campbell. Or come on a wild food walk with me. See the back inside cover for details.